THE
SHAPE
OF CHANGE

The Continued Journey of the
Digital Convergence Framework

DR. SHAWN K. SMITH

Todd Stansfield, Editor
Davina van Buren, Copy Editor

MAGNUSSON-SKOR®
PUBLISHING, LLC

Denver
www.mskor.com

Published by

MAGNUSSON-SKOR®
PUBLISHING, LLC

Magnusson-Skor Publishing
4600 S. Ulster Street Suite 1050
Denver, CO 80237
www.mskor.com

Library of Congress Control Number: 2018944196

Hardcover   ISBN 978-0-9842051-8-9
Paperback   ISBN 978-0-9842051-9-6

First Edition

For Today's Modern Leaders

" *The transition to personalized learning goes beyond any single person or initiative. It calls for districts to engage in a synchronized movement of people and solutions from every corner of our education system. It calls for Digital Convergence.*"

:: **Dr. Shawn K. Smith**, Author

CONTENTS

vi

ACKNOWLEDGEMENTS

I owe special thanks to several notable individuals who were influential in the development and publication of *The Shape of Change*. First, I would like to recognize the continued work and insight of the entire team at Modern Teacher. They continue to find new and better solutions that enable districts to scale personalized, modern learning in the classroom.

I would also like to recognize the Modern Teacher Network for its passionate commitment to creating systems that support and sustain personalized learning. The Network—including districts from across the country—continues to advance our understanding of the barriers and drivers of personalized learning. Their contributions are fueling our growing body of knowledge and illuminating a path for districts that have yet to embark on the journey toward 21st century teaching and learning.

I also would like to recognize the work of the National Council on Digital Convergence. The council—comprised of some of the most prominent minds in K–12—is bringing Digital Convergence to the forefront of national attention. National Council members include Dr. Lori Duerr; Dr. Peter Gorman; Dr. Todd Keruskin; Dr. David Miyashiro; Dr. Kelly Pew; Dr. J.R. Proctor; Dr. David Richards; Dr. Mort Sherman; and Charlene Simpson.

I would also like to thank the dedicated team of my long-time publisher, Magnusson-Skor, and my editor, Todd Stansfield. Their expertise and capabilities made this effort possible, seamless, and successful.

Lastly, I would like to acknowledge the ongoing mentorship, support, and direction of Charles L. Fred. Without you, Charles, this book would not have been possible. Thank you.

PREFACE

I sat in front of my computer considering the recent findings of more than 60 school districts using the Digital Convergence Framework. Beside the keyboard lay a notebook displaying the scrawled phrase, "The shape of change." The words came to me as I studied this latest research, which revealed patterns in the challenges, solutions, and results of districts seeking to personalize learning at scale. Through data visualization, the research presented a graphical picture of the journeys districts took in the Digital Convergence Framework—journeys that signified progress across the different drivers and stages. Interestingly, many of these graphical representations took similar forms, which helped define the interrelationships among the drivers and the district's progress in the Framework. I could, for instance, see how advancement in Leadership helped fuel progress in the other drivers, or how misalignment between Instructional Models and Modern Curriculum caused challenges. I knew these insights could inform a far more effective approach for districts already embarking on the journey toward 21st century teaching and learning, as well as those just beginning the voyage.

Over time, I decided to publish these findings in my second book about Digital Convergence. I chose *The Shape of*

Change as my title, a phrase that captured the essence of this transformation. The original idea began with the recognition that districts illustrate a shape as they work through the Digital Convergence Framework, and this shape forecasts their likelihood of success or failure. It provides a roadmap for districts that often find it difficult to understand where they stand in relation to their desired destination. It makes the process simpler, more effective, and far easier to navigate.

Part I of this book explores the concept of the shape of change. You learn the differences between effective and ineffective change as it relates to Leadership, Instructional Models, Modern Curriculum, Digital Ecosystem, and Professional Learning. This section provides you with a tool to diagnose the health of your district's progress as it journeys though the Digital Convergence Framework. You learn about the factors that prevent your district from progressing, as well as those that accelerate advancement.

Part II of this book focuses on the fundamental shift that occurs as districts transition from Stage 3 to Stage 4 of the Digital Convergence Framework. Entering Stage 4, districts have developed the conditions needed to support personalized learning at scale. Their focus in this stage shifts from developing systems to creating a workforce proficient in supporting the modern learning environment. Part II explores the effective strategies for building a proficient workforce of teachers, instructional coaches, and school-based leaders, all of whom are necessary to truly create personalized learning experiences for students.

Part III explores Stage 4 and 5 of the Digital Convergence Framework. Here, we learn the tactical action items needed to make progress in the journey toward Digital Convergence. We learn about each stage in detail across the five drivers of Convergence and gain insight into the specific action items, called success indicators, that demonstrate advancement.

This book continues the journey explored in *The New Agenda: Achieving Personalized Learning Through Digital Convergence*. As a practical guide, it offers you a ready-made tool for making your journey toward personalized learning.

THE
SHAPE
OF CHANGE

The Continued Journey of the
Digital Convergence Framework

INTRODUCTION

In 2010, something remarkable happened. For the first time ever, public high school students in a working-class suburb of Detroit received a choice. They could choose between traditional or blended learning in a small number of courses offered that year. Years later, the superintendent told me about the experience: "Blended courses simply delivered a more personalized learning experience for kids, built on their competencies, not their seat time." He continued to talk about the model, which he thought enabled students to experience more control over when, where, and how they learned, as well as the pace of their learning. He didn't focus on "blended learning," but rather, a complete *redesign* of learning. He perceived the effort more strategically than an event or pilot of 21st century education. The superintendent made a commitment to a long-term, systemic, sustainable path to ensure the redesigned learning experience eventually occurred across the district. That early group of high school students and teachers provided a glimpse into what the superintendent saw as the inevitable future.

Since publishing *The New Agenda*, I have had the privilege of watching school districts across America make the conscious decision to abandon single-point solutions in favor of Digital Convergence. I've heard stories from countless administrators as they've lead their communities toward a new vision for the classroom of the future. They've shared with me some of their greatest successes from the first three stages of the Digital

Convergence Framework, probed deeper about the work ahead, and provided invaluable feedback from the field. Their leadership is inspiring, and I continue to learn from them.

The superintendent's story is a powerful one, not only because it demonstrates that districts can develop a more effective learning environment for kids, but because it underscores the process and methodology that exists to achieve it at scale. The Digital Convergence Framework, built from a robust field research that includes the suburban district outside Detroit, serves as the platform to institutionalize the modern learning environment. Working-class suburban school districts face the same challenges as most districts across America. They operate under archaic state policies that do not support today's needs, as well as mandates by high stakes accountability systems. The district also relies on inadequate funding streams from both the state and local levels, and experiences awkward constraints on time with teachers. The list goes on. Somehow, the district overcame these obstacles. But how? Let's dive in a little deeper.

Operating within the constraints of typical late 19th and early 20th century models of education, the superintendent gave a handful of teachers autonomy over several critical factors. First, the modernization of curriculum—that meant digitizing parts of the learning experience to spare precious time needed to reach deeper levels of learning with students. It also meant leveraging the capabilities of technology to lead kids into content creation, rather than sideline them as passive consumers of information. He also innately knew that in high schools around the country, the traditional bell schedule created obstacles for teachers. He knew teachers would want to provide personalized learning pathways for their students. So, he gave them autonomy over when, where, and who needed to come to class on any given day. Yes, you read correctly: *Teachers and students made choices on when they came to class.* This allowed teachers to see certain students on Monday, others on Tuesday, everyone on Wednesday, no one on Thursday, and others on Friday. You can imagine the flexibility this created, not to mention the opportunities to engage students in authentic problem solving out in the community.

In 2010, this school district began its steady march towards modern learning. The superintendent articulated the reasons for the transition and clarified the path forward. He relentlessly focused on explaining not only *why* the transition to modern learning environments was necessary, but why it was so urgent: the sooner kids had access to personalized learning, the sooner they could begin learning more effectively, increasing their edge in today's highly competitive, technologically-focused global market. He engaged stakeholders in critical conversations about the need to redesign the learning experience at all levels of the system. And he sparked crucial conversations throughout his community. By 2012, unbeknownst to him, he worked his way through Stages 1 and 2 of the Digital Convergence Framework. In addition to starting critical conversations within his school district and the community, he armed coaches and principals with the know-how and tools to lead this work in schools.

By 2013, the superintendent was ready to launch the first teacher cohort to further build the blended learning model pioneered in 2010. Using an application process and opt-in model, 50 teachers became participants in a professional learning cohort that combined both online and in-person training. The training would cover topics on personalized learning, blended learning, new pedagogies of instruction, blended curriculum writing, classroom technologies (including a new learning management system), and rigor. All teachers would receive classroom coaching and peer support. By the end of the 2013-2014 school year, the first group of teachers successfully completed the training. By now, the district entered Stage 3 of the Digital Convergence Framework and the superintendent's focus become two-fold: first, leveraging the first cohort of teachers to drive innovation, and second, establishing the necessary systems to scale it across the district.

As the new school year began in 2014, the first cohort of teachers began to rethink their curriculum and teaching. High school teachers would spend the year transitioning their courses from traditional to blended by building out a new

5

curriculum focused on deeper student learning experiences. Elementary and middle school teachers began to rethink how technology could afford them opportunities to personalize learning pathways. By winter 2015, a handful of teachers began to emerge with new insights into how they wanted to teach their courses. Early in the process, the superintendent established a peer review system by which teachers could receive reviews from colleagues to ensure quality. He then empowered teachers with even more autonomy. As spring approached, course catalogues needed to be written and printed in preparation for the following school year. The superintendent looked to teachers ready with the knowledge and know-how to deliver their courses differently.

Meanwhile, the superintendent established several parallel readiness paths. Students and parents needed education on this new instructional approach, and the principal needed new management structures in place in the high school. The State Department of Education also needed to weigh in, and traditional policy requirements on seat time needed to be addressed and solved.

Students became eligible to take a six-week course on "How to Learn Online." It equipped them with the skills and dispositions to effectively navigate online communities, actively engage in online learning, learn about issues such as cyber-bullying, and gain confidence to take ownership of learning, both online and in-person. The superintendent also began educating parents, addressing their concerns, fears, and questions early into the process and frequently thereafter.

As summer 2015 approached, several more teachers took the leap and offered their once-traditional courses as blended. The superintendent cautiously reminded them, "Blended is not the goal. The goal is deeper learning, more engaged learning, more personalized learning. This is just the vehicle."

Those students that wanted to enroll in a blended course needed to meet two important criteria. They needed to complete the "How to Learn Online" course and their parents needed to sign a waiver acknowledging their enrollment. This waiver detailed the new freedoms they would experience, including an open campus.

By fall 2015, everything intersected, and our nation gained a shining example of K–12 public education transitioning from traditional classes to modern learning environments. Teachers were afforded the necessary autonomy needed to effectively instruct in today's world, students acquired the necessary controls over their learning, and parents recognized the types of skills their kids needed upon graduation.

Now, three years later, the school district offers more than 30 blended learning courses. As it works its way through Stage 5 of the Digital Convergence Framework, the district focuses on competency-based education. Its goal now demands building a continuum of learning from Pre–K through twelfth grade, where students can progress along the continuum as they master competencies, regardless of age or grade.

Let's take a look back at the work you engaged in through stages 1, 2, and 3 of the Digital Convergence Framework. It's important to get a sense of the organizational changes taking shape so you can better leverage them for the future.

What Happened in Stage 1

In Stage 1 of Digital Convergence, you committed to transitioning traditional classrooms into modern learning environments, at scale. You recognized the work called for leading your people through complex organizational changes that can take years. You understood that the long, slow road represented the only course that can bring about the sustained changes you want to see.

You started by forming important teams around the work and then you immediately got teams talking. You remained strategic about making sure everyone in the organization gained a voice and a sense of ownership for these conversations. You explored a diversity of opinions about blended and personalized learning, the use of learner profiles, and competency models. You experienced spirited debates about technology's role in the learning process. Stage 1 focused on facilitating conversations about the classroom of the future.

What Happened in Stage 2

In Stage 2, you made decisions about the critical conversations that took place in Stage 1. You defined for the organization what the classroom of the future should look like and you did this through a district-wide Instructional Model. You paid attention to the new skillset your workforce would need to support this new instructional model. Stage 2 focused on making key instructional and technological decisions, as well as critical organizational ones that would support these efforts.

You then transitioned into the detailed work of developing your professional learning (PL) plan. You aligned the professional learning content with your newly-defined instructional model—and in some cases, you began building your own PL content to fill in the missing pieces. Coaches became critical to this work. You started training coaches on modern learning and you rolled out a proficiency model so that you could track and monitor how your workforce continued to progress against your new instructional model. It became challenging and probably continues to be so. Sometimes it became difficult to see the bigger picture, but you kept trudging forward.

9

WHAT HAPPENED IN STAGE 3

In Stage 3, you became prepared to put in motion your strategic support plan for large scale change. You began by making sure your first wave of support—your principals and instructional coaches—acquired the necessary skills, knowledge and materials to train your workforce. You launched your first teacher cohort and you expected to learn a great deal from this first group. Your district culture began to take shape around this work, and leaders within the organization gained a shared sense of identity. Up until this point, most of the work revolved around key folks at the district creating the conditions for change to scale. You spent considerable time engaging stakeholders in readiness conversations, built a brand around the work, and prioritized a roadmap for success. Despite all this progress, don't be fooled: the work has yet to impact the classroom. Most teachers won't relate to the new brand—yet.

The good news? That's about to change.

Key Milestones from Stages 1-3

1. A Theory of Action
2. A Vision for the Classroom of the Future
3. A Brand for Convergence
4. A New Instructional Model
5. A Conceptual Digital Ecosystem
6. A Professional Learning Plan that is Aligned to Training Content
7. The Launch: School-based Leaders, Coaches and the First Teacher Cohort

In Stage 3, your district also performed its formal reflection process—a key success indicator that provided the first comprehensive analysis of your district's progress to date. To complete this success indicator, your district formally conducted interviews with key stakeholder groups, collected and synthesized the data, and developed a report that highlighted key wins and offered recommendations for improvement. This formal reflection process unveiled patterns common to all districts approaching Stage 4 of Digital Convergence—the stage when the conditions exist to create, deploy, and sustain the personalized, modern learning environment across the institution.

12

PART I:

THE SHAPE OF CHANGE

In *The New Agenda: Achieving Personalized Learning Through Digital Convergence*, we explored the first three stages of Digital Convergence—the fundamental change occurring at the school-district and national levels as our industry transitions from the traditional education model to the personalized, modern learning environment. At the school district level, Digital Convergence occurs as the district works systematically across five core drivers that include Leadership, Instructional Models, Modern Curriculum, Digital Ecosystem, and Professional Learning. At the national level, Digital Convergence occurs as district leaders, educators, and other professionals unify to share ideas, insights, collaborate, and seek solutions to establish, support, and sustain today's modern learning environment.

Now, in *The Shape of Change: The Continued Journey of the Digital Convergence Framework* we explore the changes taking place within your school district as your workforce becomes proficient with your newly-developed instructional model. The word shape literally means the condition or state of something. In this book we seek to understand the changing conditions within your organization. Taken together, our goal is to better understand the science

> **"The word shape literally means the condition or state of something and in this book we seek to understand the changing conditions within your organization."**

of change management as it relates to scaling modern learning environments. What changes need to occur to break down a century-old model of education?

Districts reaching Stage 4 experience several key transformations. During the early stages, the superintendent serves as the primary catalyst and champion for the transition from the traditional classroom model. However, as districts enter Stage 4, other stakeholders

> **"Other transformations also begin to occur, most noticeably to the district's overall identity."**

emerge as champions of the change. As early adopters of the transition, they extend the voice of the superintendent by campaigning for the change and sharing their own experiences and stories from the field. Other transformations also begin to occur, most noticeably to the district's overall identity. As your district enters Stage 4, all stakeholders are aware of the changes occurring to the district and understand the reasons driving them—no matter if they agree. Ultimately, as your district enters Stage 4, it becomes primed for change.

The transformations in your district are best illustrated through the shape of change—the common characteristics and patterns of school systems as they navigate the Digital Convergence Framework. My colleagues and I have validated these patterns based upon data from more than 50 school

15

districts using the Digital Convergence Framework. Our data demonstrate that the shape of change shows the science of convergence, and that shape constantly changes as new initiatives and actions are undertaken in each of the drivers of Digital Convergence. These common patterns provide district leaders and stakeholders with important information to guide their overall efforts.

In 2006 Tony Robbins appeared on the TED stage in California and intrigued his audience with a single sentence displayed on the screen above him: *Effective leaders have the ability to move themselves and others to action because they understand the invisible forces that shape us.* More than ever before, we are making these invisible forces within a school district visible to leaders. Through our data visualization capabilities, leaders gain valuable insights into the change process as they become wiser about the decisions they make through the path of Digital Convergence.

Let's look at a few examples.

The Shape of Change in Leadership

Figure 1 Effective Change

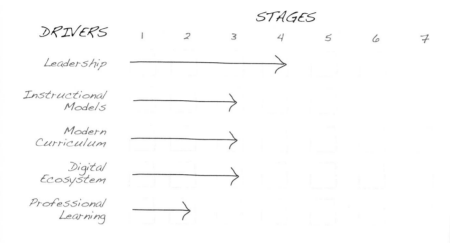

Figure 2 Less Effective Change

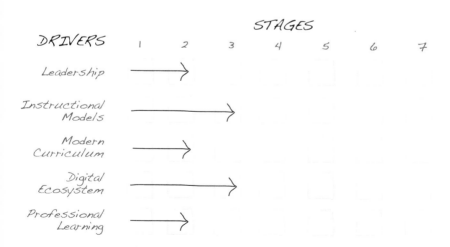

Three years ago, a large suburban school district in the American south was on the verge of a monumental change. Following a growing nationwide trend, the district wanted to maximize the potential of technology to reduce educational inequalities for impoverished students. The district, located on the outskirts of a major metropolitan city, had recently passed a $20 million technology bond, which would equip every high school student with technological devices for learning.

The district's superintendent—who had relocated from another state to accept the position just two years earlier—suddenly found himself in charge of leading the overall effort to not only integrate new technology across the institution, but to inspire a team who was navigating uncharted territory in its district.

His cabinet—which included educators, administrators, and technology professionals—recognized the need for a strategic plan that would help the organization align the necessary curricula and training that administrators and teachers would need for the new devices to be utilized effectively. Early work focused on engaging stakeholders in dialogue surrounding the need to evolve the traditional classroom model. These critical conversations

> **"Early work focused on engaging stakeholders in dialogue surrounding the need to evolve the traditional classroom model."**

built a workable action plan that would form the foundation for the work ahead: creating a compelling vision deck that articulated the key values of modern learning environments, and conducting early assessments of the district's digital content and tools. The cabinet spent months hovering between stages one and two of the digital convergence framework as they worked their way through initial success indicators.

The team experienced a few small wins along the way—forming a cross-functional team that served as the district's Digital Convergence Steering Committee, for example. As a whole, however, district stakeholders demonstrated a general lack of excitement and confidence amongst the ranks. Many educators expressed uncertainty over how the new system would impact their professional responsibilities and daily classroom routine.

Several months into the work, the district still needed to roll out the vision deck, despite completing it weeks earlier. The superintendent also needed to deliver the Message from the Top—one of the earliest and most critical steps to successfully implementing Stage 1 of Digital Convergence. Elsewhere, critical planning remained. For instance, the district still needed to make key decisions concerning the role of digital content within blended unit plans (critical success indicators in stages 2 and 3 of Modern Curriculum and Professional Learning) before an upcoming scheduled training with curriculum writers.

Lacking strong leadership and direction from the superintendent, some stakeholders began to question the role of devices in the learning process. Some wondered if traditional models of instruction provided a better teaching and learning experience, and voiced concerns that the rollout of devices without proper training and tools to support teachers would hurt student outcomes. As the curriculum training approached and pressure increased, the second-guessing among stakeholders grew louder, ultimately turning to anger toward the superintendent. Community confusion continued to grow, and six months later, the superintendent was fired.

Looking back, the early warning signs were apparent. Because the superintendent never delivered his "Message from the Top," both stakeholders and community members struggled to understand the overall direction for the transition. In this specific case, leadership lagged behind the progress of the other drivers. Digital Convergence allows districts to find their own path toward establishing a modern learning environment, but within the general structure and sequence of a proven framework. When leadership fails to lead the overall effort—especially in the early stages of digital convergence—districts experience systemic problems that can impact instruction, curriculum development, technology infrastructure, and professional learning.

The district decided to reset and start fresh from Stage One of the Digital Convergence framework. A major part of this restructuring was implementing strong leadership who would engage and inspire stakeholders. The new superintendent stepped into this challenging situation and established herself as a dedicated and thoughtful leader. She delivered a clear and focused Message from the Top, which set direction, established accountability, generated excitement and awareness, and invited community participation. Stakeholders are fully aligned in their vision, and working cohesively with clear direction to successfully implement the remaining stages of the Digital Convergence framework.

As you can glean from the story above, one such pattern is the need for leadership initiatives to drive the overall movement toward modern learning environments. Our data suggest that Leadership should consistently remain a half or full stage ahead of the other four drivers of Digital

> **"Stakeholders are fully aligned in their vision, and working cohesively with clear direction..."**

Convergence. Leadership success indicators center around establishing clear direction, communication, engagement, and vision of where you are headed. When Leadership lags behind the other drivers it increases the likelihood of causing confusion in the organization. Stakeholders invariably question if the superintendent truly supports the change and stands fully committed to leading the effort.

When confusion exists within the organization expect the following:

1. People within the organization are unclear what is ending.
2. People within the organization are unclear what is beginning.

What to do:

1. Focus on completing the Success Indicators in Leadership for Stages 1, 2, and 3.
2. Give people the proper information at the right time.
3. Communicate the vision of where you are headed.
4. Give people multiple opportunities to come to terms with the vision of the classroom of the future.

CONVERGENCE DRIVER	CENTRAL THEMES
Leadership	Compelling Vision Clear Direction Co-Construction of the Mission Shared Identity of the Work Effective and Continuous Communication

The Shape of Change in Instructional Models, Modern Curriculum, and Digital Ecosystems

Figure 3 **Effective Change**

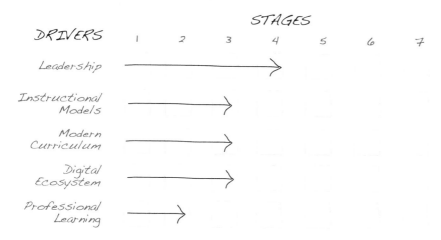

Figure 4 **Less Effective Change**

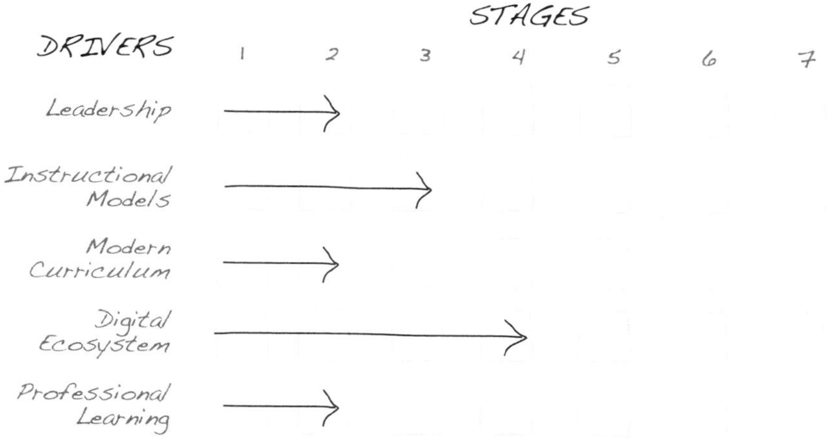

A few years ago, I traveled from Chicago to the west coast to visit a large urban school district. The plane flight took several hours, during which I recounted my conversations with the superintendent about the district's overall progress in the Digital Convergence Framework. Despite making significant progress in a short period, the district faced challenges aligning instruction and curriculum with new technology. The teams were doing great work in their respective areas—however, difficulties still stemmed from a lack of understanding about how the different teams worked and communicated best.

> "...difficulties still stemmed from a lack of understanding about how the different teams worked and communicated best."

While the technology team was in the process of designing and advancing the digital ecosystem, they met regularly with the curriculum and instruction teams to ensure complete alignment among the departments. Early into the process, it became apparent the teams faced a barrier to collaborating, one that transcended language to habits, mental models, and methods of working. While highly knowledgeable in their area of expertise, the teams lacked a shared background that could enhance working together. The technology team lacked an education background, while the curriculum and instruction departments lacked technical expertise. And the

24

highly technical nature of their disciplines made this barrier even more difficult to overcome. But the key to effective and meaningful technology integration—integration that can actually improve the teaching and learning experience—depended on the ability for these stakeholders to work together effectively.

To bridge the communication gap between the instruction/curriculum and technology teams, the school district made a bold, thoughtful decision: they moved a tenured professional in the curriculum department to the technology department. This person became the "Systems Architect," a position charged with ensuring that new technology initiatives received proper and timely input from the curriculum and instruction teams.

Because the Systems Architect didn't "speak technology," it afforded her the freedom to ask the most basic of questions. This forced the district to slow down a bit, and ensured the technology build aligned with the district's instructional needs. It also helped the instruction and curriculum teams to fully understand the impact of the proposed

> **"This one change proved both formative and immediate."**

technology, and conversely, the technology team to design with practicality and modern classrooms in mind. This one change proved both formative and immediate. Weeks after the switch, the instruction and curriculum department no longer reported feeling frustrated about the technology team's inability to listen to their needs, and vice versa. The two groups, notoriously divided, suddenly found a shared vocabulary and mode of working that resulted from the role of the Systems Architect.

While not every district has the means to make this move, placing someone with an education background on the technology team is a path worth considering. If nothing else, it forces all the teams to think differently: the technology teams know they need to explain concepts and terminology in plain terms to the Systems Architect, and the Systems Architect can expect clarity on technological concepts without feeling judged. Then, the Systems Architect can pass that information on to instruction and curriculum staff in plain language, saving everyone time and hassle.

"If nothing else, it forces all the teams to think differently..."

The experience helped reinforce my understanding of the Digital Convergence Framework. The middle three drivers of digital convergence—instruction, curriculum, and technological infrastructure—must be in complete alignment for districts to successfully transition to the modern learning environment. This means that advancement in each of these areas must remain uniform. While leadership efforts should be more advanced than the other drivers of digital convergence (as noted in the superintendent story above), instruction, curriculum, and technological infrastructure should stay near the same stage of digital convergence.

These three drivers: *Instructional Models, Modern Curriculum, and Digital Ecosystems* are commonly referred to as the **instructional and technological infrastructure of the system**. As such, they need to be lock-in-step with one another. Organizational alignment within these drivers serves as the key to building the right tools for change to occur. Our research shows a strong correlation between those districts that monitor and maintain tight alignment between these three drivers and their successes navigating the first three stages of Digital Convergence. Our data suggest these three drivers should advance at a rate of change congruent with one another.

Often, these three drivers signify vastly different departments within school systems, departments that represent silos like the

> **"Our data suggest these three drivers should advance at a rate of change congruent with one another."**

story above. School systems can achieve a natural harmony by coordinating the efforts of curriculum, instruction, and technology, which those impacted most by the changes recognize and appreciate.

In the example above, we see a common misstep from

many districts. What happens when one of the instructional or technological drivers gets too far out in front? Commonly in this case, the technology department might be driving the implementation of a new single-point solution, but failing to elicit the needed stakeholder engagement within curriculum and instruction.

When frustration exists within the organization expect the following:

1. People within the organization shut down to the changes occurring.
2. People within the organization build coalitions behind the status quo.
3. People feel less secure about their job performance.
4. Symptoms of low morale exist within the organization.

What to do:

1. Focus on the success indicators that remain uncompleted to bring all three drivers back into alignment.
2. Slow down progress for the most advanced driver(s) creating misalignment.
3. Communicate to stakeholders the need to go slower, to get things right.
4. Listen to stakeholder concerns to help connect the dots for you.

CONVERGENCE DRIVER	CENTRAL THEMES
Instructional Models	Vision of the Classroom of the Future
	Values inherent in every classroom
	Clear and concise descriptive indicators
Modern Curriculum	Blended
	Anywhere, anytime
	Adaptive
	Real time updates
	Personalized
	Relevant
	Responsive
Digital Ecosystems	Living, Breathing Habitat
	Multi-vendor
	Data Exchange
	Controlled for End User Experience

29

The Shape of Change in Professional Learning

Figure 5 **Effective Change**

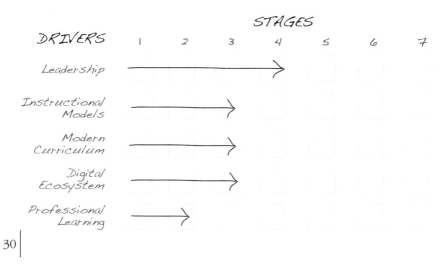

Figure 6 **Less Effective Change**

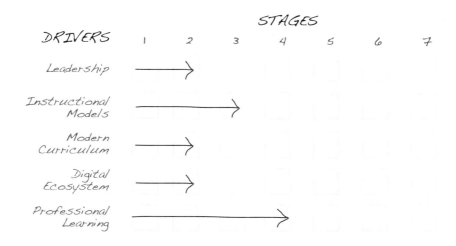

It's interesting to see how each school district customizes the Digital Convergence Framework to suit their community's unique and individual needs, but one thing every district has in common is that they follow the Framework's natural progression.

Not long ago, I had the opportunity to visit a rural, two-school district in an unincorporated community outside Waco, Texas. As I drove down, I reflected on the district's Digital Convergence journey, which started a year earlier. The district spent six months building their key messages in Leadership, Instructional Model, and Modern Curriculum. Another three months was spent meta tagging and aligning the content of their professional learning to match their instructional model and creating new, modern online and physical classroom environments. Instructional and technological models were fine-tuned using real-world feedback, and the superintendent's steady leadership and belief in the transition kept the various teams on track and progress through the Framework running smoothly.

31

> **"The district had made considerable progress since I visited and spoke about the importance of the modern learning environment."**

The district had made considerable progress since I'd last visited to speak about the importance of the modern learning environment. Together with the superintendent,

I visited each of the classrooms in the district, witnessing teachers facilitating the modern learning environment with confidence and enthusiasm. This observation data matched the proficiency data the district was tracking against their instructional model. It was compelling.

Later, in a conversation with the district superintendent, I mentioned the district's considerable progress. The superintendent told me about the district's progression through the stages of Digital Convergence, the tight alignment between the various teams, and the district's collective, cohesive vision for the modern learning environment.

Part of this alignment called for making sure that systems were in place and running smoothly before moving on to the next stage in the Framework. Once the superintendent had set the bold vision for modern learning and focused his leadership team in this direction, they shifted to building the instructional and technological infrastructure. The process proved difficult at times, but fortunately, the teams worked well together and communicated clearly when challenges or questions arose. The district is still grappling with the role of Modern Curriculum—both face-to face learning experiences as well as online—but continues to make great progress. Only

> **"...the teams worked well together and communicated clearly when challenges or questions arose."**

after the district established technological and instructional infrastructures did it move on to *Professional Learning*. This ensured what teachers were actually working on was in alignment with the district's vision for modern learning via their instructional model.

The result? A district in which everyone demonstrated a clear understanding of their roles and responsibilities, with ongoing technology education that incorporated both the district's goals and needs in conjunction with the Digital Convergence Framework.

As evidenced in this district, Professional Learning must lag behind the other drivers of digital convergence in order to be effective. Professional learning programs should only be implemented *after* establishing leadership, instruction, curriculum, and technological infrastructure.

The final driver of Digital Convergence, Professional Learning, scales the progress of the other drivers by institutionalizing change in the classroom. Like the story above, Professional Learning ensures teachers receive education that prepares them to facilitate personalized, modern learning. To do so, it draws on the fundamental conditions created by the other drivers. If the conditions remain undeveloped, Professional Learning

> "...professional learning must lag behind the other drivers of digital convergence in order to be effective."

threatens to risk institutionalizing education that doesn't reflect or cannot support personalized learning in a modern environment.

For example, when progress in Professional Learning becomes more advanced than Digital Ecosystems, teachers fail to become proficient in using the technological infrastructure to facilitate modern learning. Our research shows that when Professional Learning advances too far ahead of the other drivers, districts experience high levels of teacher complacency. When this occurs, the training may lack relevance for teachers. Teachers may feel the content of the training doesn't impact their daily workflow, doesn't add practical value, or provides no contextual relevancy to their classroom.

When complacency exists within the organization expect the following:

1. People become skeptical of the promised value of the personalized, modern learning environment.
2. People demonstrate resistance to changes and label them as "technology-focused," not "student or teacher-focused."
3. People become more invested in the status quo and fear impact of changes on student outcomes.

What to do:

1. Focus on the success indicators in the other drivers to bring progress back into alignment.

2. Align and embed the key decisions in stages 2 and 3 from Instructional Models, Modern Curriculum, and Digital Ecosystems to the professional learning training content. This will ensure relevant training and application.

3. Communicate the need to first establish the conditions for the personalized, modern learning environment before providing professional learning; define the role of professional learning and its relationship to the other drivers

4. Invite stakeholders to communicate their concerns; facilitate transparent discussions to settle nerves and address misperceptions.

CONVERGENCE DRIVER	CENTRAL THEMES
Professional Learning	Blended
	Anywhere, anytime
	Adaptive
	Relevant and Contextual
	Built on a Clearly Defined Proficiency Model
	Personalized

By now, you've become familiar with the salient themes in each driver and what happened within each driver. The full chart is listed here.

CONVERGENCE DRIVER	CENTRAL THEMES
Leadership	Compelling Vision Clear Direction Co-Construction of the Mission Shared Identity of the Work Effective and Continuous Communication
Instructional Models	Vision of the Classroom of the Future Values inherent in every classroom Clear and concise descriptive indicators
Modern Curriculum	Blended Anywhere, anytime Adaptive Real time updates Personalized Relevant Responsive
Digital Ecosystems	Living, Breathing Habitat Multi-vendor Data Exchange Controlled for End User Experience
Professional Learning	Blended Anywhere, anytime Adaptive Relevant and Contextual Built on a Clearly Defined Proficiency Model Personalized

The Importance of Goal Cycles

Digital Convergence is not an event, but a long-term, ongoing commitment that requires systemic coordination from stakeholders across the organization. The Digital Convergence Framework contains 110 success indicators across five drivers and seven stages, presenting challenging work for the district that can seem daunting and overwhelming for some. As with any long-term challenge, success depends on breaking down work into manageable parts, which provides the benefits of increasing focus on one aspect of change, while at the same time motivating people psychologically through the power of achievement. Compartmentalizing the effort creates the conditions for positive momentum, as stakeholders recognize their power to help the district move closer to the personalized, modern learning environment. Unlike asking your teams to take on what can seem an endless and overwhelming effort, this different approach enables them to embrace a more practicable outlook of the change effort, focus on manageable tasks, and build confidence and motivation over time through success.

This crucial approach begins with setting goal cycles, or incremental periods devoted to setting and completing objectives associated with the Digital Convergence Framework. Goal cycles ensure people stay focused on the present, while limiting the noise of self-doubt and competing priorities natural to any long-term effort. Importantly, goal cycles enhance project management efforts by simplifying priorities and tasks. Those working on a goal understand the work they need to complete and their key responsibilities, which would otherwise leave them with a vague understanding if left uncontextualized. Goal cycles also enhance stakeholder involvement by increasing their ownership of and participation in the process. As we explored, Stage 3 called for reflecting on and celebrating the progress of the district in the journey toward modern learning via the Digital Convergence Framework. A necessary and important success indicator, this occurred at the district level. Entering Stage 4, this process of recognition and reflection becomes distributed across teams and individuals collectively working toward modern learning.

"Those working on a goal understand the work they need to complete and their key responsibilities..."

Goal cycles enable individuals to see, own, and celebrate the success of completing a success indicator. For instance, stakeholders working on Modern Curriculum gain the ability to celebrate each success indicator they complete, increasing their satisfaction, engagement, and motivation to continue the work. This represents an important characteristic of Stage 4. The movement through Digital Convergence becomes an effort led by stakeholders throughout the district, who become champions of the change alongside the superintendent.

The process of goal cycles begins with "chunking"—or organizing—the work of Digital Convergence in six to 12-week increments for each of the drivers. It calls for setting a manageable number of tasks and activities in that timeframe tied directly to success indicators to ensure goals remain specific, measurable, attainable, and realistic.

The value of goal cycles begins with this focus on length of time—1.5 to 3 months—which leads to change over time that steadily becomes more noticeable. Celebrating key milestones and progress serves as an essential task to ensure that stakeholders expand their focus from the length of time within each Goal Cycle to recognize the changes occurring around them. This kind of celebration can take a variety of forms and doesn't necessarily call for a district-wide event. Rather, it can take the form of verbal recognition among a small team of individuals working on a driver of Digital Convergence. Or it can take the shape of an

> **"Celebrating key milestones and progress serves as an essential task..."**

email from district leadership, congratulating the champions of change on their progress. Or it can mean a newsletter or tweet from district or school-based leadership. The medium for recognizing change is less important than ensuring that it occurs consistently and continually over time.

This broad movement only increases the need and importance for the superintendent to continue to recognize success at the district-level. This enables stakeholders to see beyond the immediate focus of their goal cycles to recognize how their work fits into the broader effort of Digital Convergence. They can see, for instance, how the work of Modern Curriculum influences that of Digital Ecosystems, and vice versa. And it becomes increasingly important for several reasons. For one, it enhances a sense of community among stakeholders who may otherwise become isolated by their focused, targeted work within one department at the district office. It also ensures that these champions develop and sustain an appropriate understanding of Digital Convergence as a system of five drivers, rather than focusing on one driver alone (Leadership, Instructional Models, Modern Curriculum, Digital Ecosystems, or Professional Learning). Additionally, recognizing progress also creates awareness around the important changes taking place at the district-level.

> **"Additionally, recognizing progress also creates awareness around the important changes taking place at the district-level."**

Recognizing past success also serves as an opportune time to prepare for and focus on future work remaining. While important to celebrate progress, equally important is maintaining the focus and motivation of stakeholders. Naturally, they feel a sense of renewed commitment and motivation when reflecting on past success, making it the perfect moment to catalyze their momentum and drive for upcoming work. Establishing this cadence—wherein stakeholders set goal cycles, complete tasks, recognize their success, and renew their drive for the next goal cycle— makes the long-term process of Digital Convergence not only manageable, but highly effective. Document and make transparent the goal cycle process. It can take discipline, but is well worth the results.

41

42

Part II:

The Shift:

From district culture to the classroom of the future: building a proficiency tipping point

Entering Stages 4 and 5

Stages 1-3 intentionally focused on creating the conditions that effectively enable change to take shape across the district. Central to this idea became the focus on building and strengthening the school district culture. School-based leaders facilitated culture conversations around Digital Convergence and the need to transform teaching and learning. The district developed plans to continually communicate the work of Digital Convergence through various internal and external outlets. Discussions about student outcomes began to extend beyond quantitative state assessments. And overall, the district began to redesign existing infrastructure, creating the optimal conditions for implementing modern learning across the organization.

1	2	3
Begin critical conversations among stakeholders	Make key instructional & technological decisions to scale changes.	Empower early adopters to champion the cultural shift to modern learning at scale.

In Stage 4, the district experiences an intentional shift in focus from the district to the classroom. The key conditions exist to institutionalize the work of Digital Convergence, and this begins by building a proficiency model that provides teachers with the knowledge and confidence to facilitate the modern learning environment. Changes manifest in the classroom and refine over time as teachers become proficient in the new instructional model.

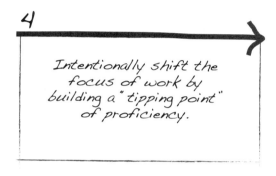

4

Intentionally shift the focus of work by building a "tipping point" of proficiency.

THE PROFICIENCY MODEL

People remain the greatest asset of any enterprise. Hal Rosenbluth, author of the once-controversial book *The Customer Comes Second: And Other Secrets of Exceptional Service*, illustrates the power of investing in human capital. At a time when everyone subscribed to the phrase "the customer is always right," Rosenbluth took the controversial stance that employees, not customers, were the secret to success in business. He committed to investing in his people, and as a result, his company, Rosenbluth Travel, grew from $20 million to $1.5 billion at the time his book was published in 1992. As a part of this investment, Rosenbluth focused on employee training, recognizing its close connection to engagement and performance. After all, well-trained employees are naturally better able

"Training is as necessary as a road map in an unfamiliar place."

to perform their role, which boosts confidence, satisfaction, and engagement in their work. Rosenbluth writes, "Training is as necessary as a road map in an unfamiliar place. Why let your people take a wrong turn, when providing them with information will lead them to the best place? Providing them with the best information possible will get them there quickly, accurately, and with pride."

Over time, Rosenbluth's point of view caught the attention of leaders around the country. Today, his once-controversial stance now represents a mainstream belief universally accepted, with the phrase "the customer is always right" debunked by the mantra "invest in your people." His point of view shifted the center of gravity in business from consumer to employee. Organizations now recognize the need to invest in their people—not only creating engaging cultures, but making learning an ongoing emphasis. As Rosenbluth recognized, the most successful companies believe the highest performing employee is the knowledgeable worker, since

46

knowledge creates the conditions for engagement, confidence, and satisfaction. Consider examples of some of today's Fortune 500 companies. Quicken Loans, a national mortgage lender named to *Forbes* magazine's "100 Best Companies To Work For" list, provides the average employee with 350 hours of training annually. Stryker, which makes medical devices, provides employees with more than 100 hours of training on an average each year. And Hyatt, the global hotel chain, takes a similar approach, providing nearly 100 hours of training on average annually. These companies serve as a few of the many examples of organizations making their people and learning priorities— which ultimately creates the conditions for exceptional performance and customer experience.

Employees serve a vital role in every industry and business, but perhaps none more so than in K–12 education. Consider the nature of our work and the "customers" to whom we serve. Unlike retail, the implications of poor performance do not merely mean inconvenience or a poor shopping experience. Rather, they impact the lives of students, making it more difficult to succeed later in life,

> **"Employees serve a vital role in every industry and business, but perhaps none more so than in K–12 education."**

which reduces the quality of life. When truly considering the value of employees in K–12 education, our ability to perform remains paramount. And as a result, so does our commitment to ensuring we get the attention, support, and training we need to succeed in our respective roles.

While training always plays an important role, its importance increases in the transition toward Digital Convergence. Digital Convergence calls for adopting new technology, pedagogies, mental models, and perceptions about what K–12 education can and should look like. It calls for rewiring and redefining what it means to live and work as an educator in our school systems. To put it simply, a lot can go wrong without adequate, sustained, and effective training. A significant knowledge gap exists that our teacher workforce must gain the ability to close, which requires our ongoing focus and commitment. Failing this, we can only expect problems in the form of frustration, dissatisfaction, disengagement, and ultimately poor performance. We can only expect worse student outcomes as we fail to answer society's call to produce graduates who can meet the challenges of our modern day. We can and must ensure our teachers gain the knowledge and confidence to facilitate the personalized, modern learning environment.

> **"To put it simply, a lot can go wrong without adequate, sustained, and effective training."**

So, how do we ensure our teachers become proficient? How do we build a proficiency model that scales this effort across our workforce? First, let's define proficiency. Charles Fred, one of the leading minds when it comes to workforce proficiency and adult education, defines proficiency as "the ability of an individual worker to produce the promised value to customers" (41). In the context of the 21st century classroom, proficiency means the

> **"The more time we spend practicing a task, the more proficient we become in completing it."**

ability for teachers to facilitate learning that prepares students to succeed in our modern world. It calls for a different skillset than the traditional classroom; teachers must embrace a new role that empowers students to drive their own learning, a role that combines new pedagogies, curriculum, and technology for new results.

Proficiency is not an established marker; rather, it becomes a dynamic outcome of the attention, energy, and experience one develops over time. The more time we spend practicing a task, the more proficient we become in completing it. In his book *Breakaway*, Fred defines three levels of proficiency: literacy, fluency, and mastery. According to Fred, literacy is the ability to articulate knowledge in the context of one's job... fluency is the ability to perform a task with ease...[fluency] can be attained only through actual practice and application. Fluency marks the threshold level of proficiency required for the essential function of most jobs...mastery is achieved with additional experience, when one acquires true expertise. This level is generally beyond what is necessary to deliver value to customers and therefore represents an unnecessary goal for training and development.

He writes that the level of proficiency is a crucial consideration depending on the importance of the task. Some tasks call for higher levels of proficiency than others, and vice versa. Considering the valuable work of teachers, we should strive to ensure they become fluent in all tasks necessary to facilitate personalized, modern learning experiences. This ensures that teachers establish a strong foundation of knowledge and confidence from which to develop expertise and master the modern learning environment over time.

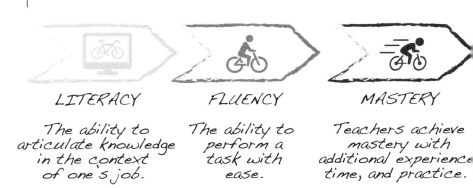

LITERACY
The ability to articulate knowledge in the context of one's job.

FLUENCY
The ability to perform a task with ease.

MASTERY
Teachers achieve mastery with additional experience, time, and practice.

The question then becomes, how do we build teacher proficiency across your district and at scale? The answer lies in being thoughtful about developing a proficiency tipping point.

A Proficiency Tipping Point

In his book *The Tipping Point: How Little Things Can Make a Big Difference*, Malcolm Gladwell writes, "The tipping point is that magic moment when an idea, trend, or social behavior crosses a threshold, tips and spreads like wildfire." He uses this concept to describe the moment when something—a disease, a social movement, a major evolution that alters life on a considerable scale—becomes an epidemic. As the title of his book suggests, the tipping point serves as a phenomenon where the slightest details carry significant implications. So, what do we mean by building a proficiency tipping point? The answer lies in Gladwell's "three rules of a Tipping Point": the Law of the Few, the Stickiness Factor, and the Power of Context. Gladwell's "three rules of the Tipping Point" have enormous implications for the transition from the traditional classroom to the personalized modern learning environment. So how can we apply this to the movement toward personalized, modern learning environments? How can Gladwell's "three rules of the Tipping Point" inform how we spread the social epidemic of transitioning our classrooms into the modern age?

Gladwell's Law of the Few, for instance, says that epidemics begin approaching the tipping point when a few actors catalyze their movement. Infectious diseases become epidemics not because of the actions of an entire population, but because of the behaviors of a few. Social movements don't emerge because a large group decides to coalesce simultaneously around a principle; rather, we can trace their origin to a few individuals who ignited the need for social change. In terms of proficiency, we see the Law of the Few in providing the professional learning to our instructional coaches, school-based leaders, and first teacher cohorts to create early champions of the movement, champions proficient and capable to galvanize the broader movement toward Digital Convergence. This cohort of teachers has long been your typical go-to folks for any type of change you've had to endure.

Gladwell defines the Stickiness Factor as the evolution of an infectious agent that creates the conditions for an epidemic. For example, in the context of social epidemics, the infectious agent takes the form of messages. The more "sticky" the messages, the more unforgettable they become, and the more likely the epidemic spreads until it eventually tips. Just think of the lyrics to the most popular songs of a generation—lyrics that people of all different ethnicities, demographics, characteristics, and lifestyle behaviors can recall with stunning clarity. Or think of how people can recite the favorite lines of a movie, of poetry, of fiction. Gladwell writes, "The Stickiness Factor says that there are specific ways of making a contagious message memorable; there are relatively simple changes in the presentation and structuring of information that can make a big difference in how much of an impact it makes" (29). For the proficiency tipping point, we see the Stickiness Factor in the crucial messages from the superintendent, communicating not only the need and importance of this work, but the key wins and progress achieved in the process. Moreover, we see the Stickiness Factor within the first teacher cohort. It is evidenced

"...epidemics need the right environment and context in which to occur."

by their enthusiasm and excitement as they demonstrate the application of new instructional strategies in their classrooms.

Lastly is Gladwell's Power of Context, which says epidemics need the right environment and context in which to occur. Gladwell writes of the Power of Context "that human beings are a lot more sensitive to their environment than they may seem." He explores the phenomenon of people coming to the aid of others when under duress. The more people who witness an event, such as a stabbing or heart attack, the less likely people provide assistance. For whatever reason, people become less inclined to intervene when others are around, underscoring the effect of context on behavior. For K–12 education, we see the Power of Context in the conditions for personalized, modern learning to occur, conditions created through progress in the first three stages of Digital Convergence. As districts advance in the Digital Convergence Framework, they see the emergence of new champions beyond the superintendent, which drives the power of context through social significance, increasing the likelihood of galvanizing others to embrace the effort and tip the scale.

The proficiency tipping point doesn't represent random, isolated success, but the outcome of a substantial effort over a year in the making. Over the last year, as you worked your way through the first three stages of Digital Convergence, you created a powerful context for change to occur at scale. This context became co-created by investing in and engaging your stakeholders along the way. A shared sense of identity emerged around the transformation of the district into a modern learning environment and your brand shaped your district culture.

> "The proficiency tipping point doesn't represent random, isolated success, but the outcome of a substantial effort over a year in the making."

You created the conditions for something to tip by leveraging the law of a few, ensuring a stickiness factor, and setting a powerful context for change. Now the question is, what do you want to tip? It's somewhat of a rhetorical question. The answer, of course, is a proficient workforce skilled in your newly defined instructional model. As described above, we've defined proficiency in our proficiency model and aligned it to your district's instructional model. It's now time to harness the power of a few and tip the proficiency scale in your district.

Professional Learning Goals

Your district uses its instructional model developed in stages 2 and 3 (success indicators 18 and 41) to write goals from which to determine and measure proficiency for teachers. These goals ultimately establish the target for teachers to gain the knowledge, confidence, and competencies to successfully facilitate the personalized, modern learning environment. So, how do you write goal statements that meet the needs of your district and reflect your instructional model?

To begin, start by identifying the domains or quadrants of your instructional model, which you developed in Stage 2. These domains represent the key characteristics that define your vision of the modern learning environment. For each quadrant, identify the desired ability teachers need to support certain characteristics of the modern learning environment. If the modern learning environment provides student-centered learning, for example, what abilities do teachers need to successfully facilitate it? This ultimately identifies the desired outcome of professional learning, which should build the knowledge and competencies to ensure teachers can facilitate all aspects of the instructional model, and therefore the modern learning environment.

Goal statements should begin with what teachers need to accomplish in the new instructional model. Therefore, each goal should begin with the phrase: *Teachers will . . .*

Then, the goal statement should identify the appropriate action associated with the domain. Do teachers need to provide, create, or assess something? Or do they need to perform another task? This second component of the goal statement defines the action.

Teachers will be able to provide . . .

Teachers will be able to create . . .

Teachers will be able to assess . . .

Next, the goal statement should define the outcomes teachers must be able to produce relative to the domain. If one domain calls for a student-centered learning environment, then what ability do teachers need to accomplish to support the student-centered learning environment?

Teachers will be able to provide their students with a supportive, student-centered learning environment . . .

The final task for creating a goal statement is to specify the extent, whenever applicable. In this case, you need to define to what extent teachers must achieve the outcome whenever applicable.

Teachers will be able to provide their students with a supportive, student-centered learning environment, both in the classroom and online.

You finished your first goal statement. Now, you continue the process by writing one goal for each of the other domains.

Once you develop your goals, you can develop and align professional learning that focuses on making teachers proficient in the competencies needed to support the domains of the instructional model. Together, the instructional model, goals, and professional learning create alignment that enable your district to quickly build the proficiency tipping point and scale the modern learning environment effectively and sustainably.

Let's review an example of an instructional model and goals to solidify our understanding:

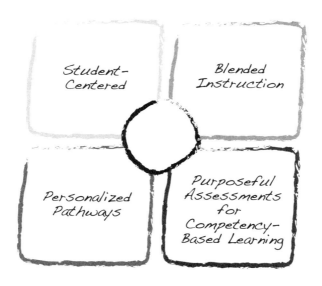

Imagine the previous graphic illustrates your district's instructional model. Following are sample goal statements that you may develop for your district:

Goal 1 - *Teachers will be able to provide their students with a supportive, student-centered learning environment, both in the classroom and online.*

Goal 2 - *Teachers will be able to create best-practice blended lessons using a range of effective pedagogical methods.*

Goal 3 - *Teachers will be able to effectively assess their students' learning, and use those assessments to revise instruction and provide more personalized learning options.*

Goal 4 - *Teachers will be able to personalize the learning experience for each student, leveraging their unique learner profiles and providing freedom over their time, pace, path, and pace of learning.*

Notice that each goal statement contains the three components we explored previously. "*Teachers will*" starts the goal, followed by the ability they need to acquire, followed by the outcome they need to achieve and to what extent.

Goal statements remain a vital condition to reaching proficiency on any level, not to mention the proficiency tipping point. As such, it should gain the emphasis and consideration of your district as you move to institutionalize your instructional model in your classrooms.

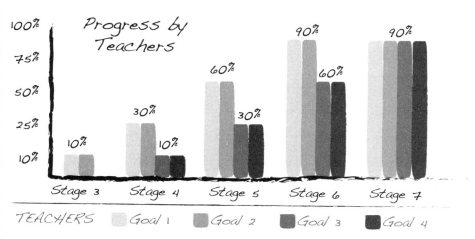

Progress by Teachers

Teacher Proficiency –

Goals 1 & 2 of District's Instructional Model

Stage 3: 10% of workforce becomes proficient in Goals 1 & 2

Stage 4: 30% of workforce becomes proficient in Goals 1 & 2

Stage 5: 60% of workforce becomes proficient in Goals 1 & 2

TIPPING POINT GOALS 1 & 2

Stage 6: 90% of workforce becomes proficient in Goals 1 & 2

Teacher Proficiency –

Goals 3 & 4 of District's Instructional Model

Stage 4: 10% of workforce becomes proficient in Goals 3 & 4

Stage 5: 30% of workforce becomes proficient in Goals 3 & 4

Stage 6: 60% of workforce becomes proficient in Goals 3 & 4

TIPPING POINT GOALS 3 & 4

Stage 7: 90% of workforce becomes proficient in Goals 3 & 4

SHAPE OF CHANGE

So, what happens to the Shape of Change when districts reach the proficiency tipping point? It displays a common pattern recognizable in the Digital Convergence Framework. To illustrate, let's review the evolution of the Shape of Change as districts approach Stage 4. At this point, the Shape of Change should take the form of an "S."

This becomes evident when we examine the key concepts of Digital Convergence, which we explore in *The New Agenda: Achieving a Personalized Approach Toward Digital Convergence.* The first concept, "Setting the Tone from the Top," says that change begins when leadership sets the direction, tone, and commitment toward an objective, just as President John F. Kennedy did when he set the goal of landing a man on the moon by the end of the decade in the 1960s. The next concept, "Irony of Instruction (it's about the learner)" says that students all learn differently based on thousands of unique neuropathways. Personalized, modern learning calls for instructional models, curriculum, and technology that enables students to learn according to their highly personalized needs. Next is the third concept,

> **"...change begins when leadership sets the direction, tone, and commitment toward an objective..."**

"Crowdsource Content, Not Competencies," which says that districts must establish the competencies they want students to acquire. This provides a framework for choosing appropriate content for curriculum, which is now more essential than ever given the amount of content shared and available via the internet. The fourth concept, "A Living Breathing Habitat," says that districts must create an integrated ecosystem that supports and integrates a network of multi-vendor solutions. Ultimately, it entails a significant effort for districts, which "must work to build their own ecosystem organically and develop the internal processes, support systems, and infrastructure to sustain the ecosystem over time." The final concept, "Inquiry, Then Proficiency, Not Attendance," says that teachers need to receive the same type of instruction they are expected to facilitate in the modern learning environment, instruction that builds proficiency through deep levels of inquiry and then measures that proficiency rather than mere attendance at the training.

> "...teachers need to receive the same type of instruction they are expected to facilitate in the modern learning environment..."

61

All five concepts illustrate the reason the Shape of Change initially takes the form of an "S." Leadership, at the top of the Digital Convergence Framework, should remain at the forefront of progress—recall that Leadership should always remain a half or full stage ahead of the other drivers. Following Leadership, the drivers of Instructional Models, Modern Curriculum, and Digital Ecosystem should remain relatively aligned. Lastly, Professional Learning should demonstrate the least advancement of the drivers, which set the conditions for successful learning to occur.

Over time, however, this shape changes as Professional Learning becomes more aligned with the instructional and technological drivers of Digital Convergence. Once districts reach the proficiency tipping point, progress in Professional Learning should become relatively uniform with Instructional Models, Modern Curriculum, and Digital Ecosystems. And consider why: at this point, the district already developed the instructional and technological capacity for personalized learning, established the competencies from which to crowdsource content, and created a living ecosystem of digital resources. With these conditions set, it becomes necessary that teachers reach a level of proficiency consistent with the instructional and technological arenas in which they perform.

CHANGING SHAPE, THE INVERTED S

But what happens beyond the proficiency tipping point? What happens as teachers not only become fluent in the modern learning environment, but begin to master it? While our research is limited in this respect, given that Digital Convergence remains a new and emerging science, my colleagues and I believe Professional Learning may advance ahead of the other drivers *at times.* In essence, this would invert the "S" shape pattern we see when districts reach

"...teachers face the shortest cycle time to reach the proficiency level of mastery..."

Stage 4. As teachers become more proficient in facilitating the modern learning environment, they likely begin to drive changes to Instructional Models, Modern Curriculum, and Digital Ecosystems through their expertise. Unlike other stakeholders, teachers face the shortest cycle time to reach the proficiency level of mastery, given the nature of their role, which naturally provides them the most exposure to, involvement with, and expertise in the modern learning environment. It only makes sense that they naturally become drivers of enhancements and improvements through their discoveries. Teachers may recommend changes to any of the instructional and technological drivers of Digital Convergence. This would require Leadership to catch up to the advancements made in Professional Learning, followed by the other drivers, while progress in Professional Learning fails to advance until the system catches up. Then, as the conditions are set for the change to occur (first through Leadership and then through the other drivers), those changes should be scaled through

63

Professional Learning until the driver becomes more aligned with the others.

The Shape of Change follows this general pattern, but the pattern itself changes as the district becomes more advanced in the Digital Convergence Framework. As the district adopts new technology and enhances its instructional model and curriculum, the shape of change resets to its initial "S" shape pattern to enable the district to establish the instructional and technological infrastructure before scaling the change to the district. The shape also changes year over year with employee turnover. As new employees enter the district the tipping point will rest itself. Yet as the district becomes more advanced, not only technologically and instructionally, but mentally and culturally, the speed with which the shape of change occurs increases dramatically. This means the cycle time for Professional Learning to catch pace with the other drivers shortens, as professional learning is quickly updated to reflect new innovations and enhancements in the district.

"As new employees enter the district the tipping point will rest itself."

As districts work in Stages 4 and 5, the Shape of Change begins to emerge as more teachers, instructional coaches, and school-based leaders become workforce proficient in the new instructional model. Yet up until now, our focus has largely remained on teachers in professional learning. It's time to turn our attention to other stakeholders crucial to making professional learning effectively occur.

INSTRUCTIONAL COACHES TO SUPPORT PROFICIENCY

Instructional coaches serve a vital role in ensuring teachers become proficient in the modern learning environment. Consider the value they bring from a social, psychological, and instructional standpoint. On the one hand, coaches serve as champions of the movement, extending and reinforcing the voice and vision of leadership in their personal interactions with teachers. For instance, coaches continue to talk about Digital Convergence and the importance of transforming teaching and learning. They increase the social significance of the change, making it more important to commit to the movement and invest in the behaviors that promote modern learning experiences. Coaches also help ease the perceived burden of the effort by providing teachers with support and attention. For instance, they allay anxieties about the transition for teachers who may feel less technology-oriented. They also quiet the self-doubt and resistance that may otherwise cause teachers to fight the transition. And most importantly, coaches help provide teachers with the knowledge and confidence to meet the challenges of the personalized, modern learning environment. They not only provide at-the-elbow support, but they help deliver the appropriate instruction when and where teachers need it. Coaches provide teachers with instruction using the same instructional models and technology that the new environment demands of teachers. Coaches facilitate learning just as teachers should in the modern classroom, enabling teachers to drive how they learn. As a result, instructional coaches not only help provide teachers with the learning they need, but, by the nature of their work, they provide a real-life example of the new role teachers must adopt.

For instructional coaches to add the most value, they must serve as exemplars of facilitating the modern learning environment. It also remains important that they hold significant social standing in the organization and are well-respected within the organization. And of course, these individuals must demonstrate a strong understanding and sense of commitment to the important work of Digital Convergence.

Just as teachers received professional learning on the district's new instructional model, broken down into goals 1, 2, 3, and 4, this should serve as the focus of instructional coaches. Unlike teachers, however, the tipping point remains different for instructional coaches, both in the percentage needed to reach workforce proficiency, as well as the stage in which stakeholders reach it. While teachers reach the proficiency tipping point in Stage 6 and 7, instructional coaches reach it in Stage 6. However, a sizeable percentage of instructional coaches become proficient in Stage 3 and 4.

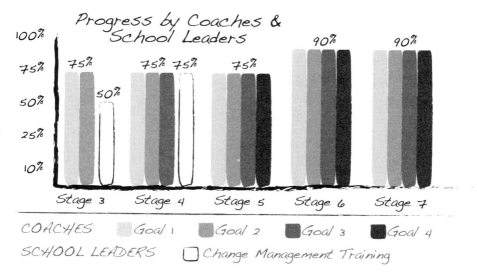

Instructional Coach Proficiency –

Goals 1 & 2 of District's Instructional Model

Stage 3: 75% of workforce becomes proficient in Goals 1 & 2

TIPPING POINT GOALS 1 & 2

Stage 6: 90% of workforce becomes proficient in all PL goals

Instructional Coach Proficiency –

Goals 3 & 4 of District's Instructional Model

Stage 4: 75% of workforce becomes proficient in Goal 3

Stage 5: 75% of workforce becomes proficient in Goal 4

TIPPING POINT GOALS 3 & 4

Stage 6: 90% of workforce becomes proficient in all PL goals

School-based Leaders Ready to Lead Change

School-based leaders also play a vital role in tipping the proficiency scale. For teachers to successfully gain the knowledge and confidence to succeed, school-based leaders must become prepared to lead the effort in their schools. Like instructional coaches, school-based leaders create the social, psychological, and instructional conditions needed to truly build a proficient workforce. From a social and psychological standpoint, school-based leaders provide the direction, transparency, and support needed to resolve resistance to change, alleviate anxieties, and emphasize leadership's commitment to supporting educators through the transition. They do this through their culture conversations with teachers, as well as their unplanned interactions with them. As leaders, these individuals invite educators to take ownership of the movement, and foster inspiration through encouragement and leadership. Instructionally, school-based leaders reinforce the important behaviors the modern learning environment demands by emphasizing its importance during each interaction. The latter remains important by ensuring educators perceive the commitment of their leaders to the modern learning environment, which in turn increases their

"...school-based leaders must become prepared to lead the effort in their schools."

investment. It also creates more transparency around the behaviors educators must acquire to ensure students achieve the best outcomes.

For school-based leaders to add the most value, they must truly stand committed to the modern learning environment. They must gain the knowledge and confidence to talk intelligibly and convincingly about Digital Convergence (the process used to scale modern learning) and the need to transform teaching and learning. They must also acquire extensive knowledge about the barriers and drivers of Digital Convergence (the overall process). And school-based leaders must learn the instructional behaviors that the modern learning environment calls for, behaviors that facilitate rigor and 21st century skills, but that also put the student in charge of the learning process.

CHANGE MANAGEMENT

While teachers and instructional coaches focus on professional learning goals, training for school-based leaders focuses on change management. Professional learning in this context centers on building a shared understanding of the change process and the emotions that people naturally experience. Today, there remains no better resource for understanding change management than the work of William

Bridges in his book *Managing Transitions: Making the Most of Change*. Bridges writes of three phases of transition people naturally and consistently experience when confronted with evolution. Understanding these patterns of emotions inform better approaches and solutions for helping guide people through the change process, making it less burdensome and more successful. Bridges' work serves as the exact solution school-based leaders need to adopt to shepherd their schools from the traditional classroom to the modern learning environment.

First Order Versus Second Order Change

To truly manage change effectively, school-based leaders must understand two fundamental types that pose dramatically different implications. They represent *first order* and *second order change*. First order change is the kind we most frequently experience. It represents the easiest change to implement, often occurs on a small scale, and can easily be reverted to status quo. We see first order change when our department institutes a new protocol designed to improve some aspect of our performance, whether efficiency, effectiveness, productivity, so forth. Often, first order change doesn't require new learning, and it occurs under the general system that perpetuates the status quo. First order change in the traditional classroom model doesn't require a departure from a teacher-centered system of instruction. Rather, it calls for improvements or enhancements to the same general processes of working.

Second order change, on the other hand, carries far more significant implications. It necessitates a complete overhaul of the current system. It calls for a departure from the mental models, behaviors, and beliefs that perpetuate the status quo. And in doing so, it upsets an entire order of balance that launch stakeholders into a frenzy of mixed and often negative emotions. Second order change necessitates new solutions and approaches to old problems. It requires new learning to help people embrace an entirely new realm.

Let's be clear, the modern learning environment calls for second order change. While a necessary transformation, it inevitably becomes disruptive, disorienting, and difficult for those who inhabit our school systems. As such, it remains vitally important that we understand how to ease the burden and make it as navigable as possible.

Bridges' the Three Phases of Change

In *Managing Transitions: Making the Most of Change*, Bridges defines three phases of transition that people navigate during any change initiative. They serve to simplify the highly complex emotional journey people experience, which Bridges calls out when he writes "there is an ending, then a neutral zone, and only then a new beginning. But those phases are not separate stages with clear boundaries. As the figure suggests, the three phases of transition are more like curving, slanting, overlapping strata than like sequential stages."

> **"...the ending occurs with the departure from the traditional classroom model."**

The first phase serves as "the ending" of the status quo. Bridges defines this phase as "Letting go of the old ways and the old identity people had...[It represents] the time when you need to help people to deal with their losses." People in this phase experience fear, overreaction, grief, and confusion. They demonstrate fear because they are afraid of losing the comfort of the status quo. They overreact because they feel the loss as a sign of something larger to come. They undergo the seven stages of grief because they have lost something truly valuable to them. And they are confused about what to expect of the new world into which they are thrust.

In the context of the modern learning environment, the ending occurs with the departure from the traditional classroom model. Educators, students, parents, administrators, and other stakeholders are forced to let go of habits and identities deeply rooted and entrenched in their psychology. It calls for

72

school-based leaders to address fears by acknowledging losses openly and sympathetically, and presenting closure to some aspects of the traditional classroom model. And it calls for addressing overreactions by recognizing the losses still to come; specifically, the aspects of the current system that will end and continue. This phase necessitates expecting and accepting that stakeholders will experience the stages of grief. They should be allowed time to reach acceptance. And it calls for giving people the information they need to overcome confusion – when and where they need it most. Communication should never be treated as an event or episode, but an ongoing need to solidify and reinforce understanding. It is an important success indicator in every stage of the Digital Convergence Framework, referenced as Message from the Top.

The second phase represents what Bridges labels "The Neutral Zone." He defines this phase as "Going through an in-between time when the old is gone but the new isn't fully operational. We call this time the 'neutral zone': it's when the critical psychological realignments and repatternings take place." Here, people experience a range of emotions. They feel anxiety, which invariably rises as people become doubtful, resentful, fatigued, and overwhelmed by the

> **"Communication should never be treated as an event or episode, but an ongoing need to solidify and reinforce understanding."**

change. They demonstrate weakness as they experience distrust, become disengaged, and revert to bad habits and suboptimal performance. They also demonstrate cognitive overload as they appear bombarded with information and mixed messages that confuse priorities and cause them to overlook tasks. And more broadly, people become polarized and hold opposing viewpoints about the change.

> "...the neutral zone occurs as stakeholders begin the transition from the traditional classroom to the modern learning environment."

For the modern learning environment, the neutral zone occurs as stakeholders begin the transition from the traditional classroom to the modern learning environment. Stakeholders are forced to begin embracing the new reality of the change. And it calls for school-based leaders to embrace a different approach. They must, for instance, focus on protecting people from unnecessary changes and prioritizing the efforts to enhance clarity. They must also review policies and procedures to create temporary systems that eliminate ambiguity and create manageable rules that support the transition. But it doesn't end there. Leaders need to manage and control messages to ensure stakeholders receive the right information at the appropriate time consistently. They must also become creative and enhance the current processes that educate people in the new model to ensure they are no longer

74

overloaded. And lastly, school-based leaders need a collection of individuals who can manage the transition and monitor its progress, ultimately helping the organization transition to next phase.

The third phase represents the "new beginning," or the full implementation of the new model. Bridges defines this phase as "Coming out of the transition and making a new beginning. This is when people develop the new identity, experience the new energy, and discover the new sense of purpose that make the change begin to work." In this phase, people experience ambivalence, fear reality, and resist the transition. They demonstrate uncertainty over the new commitment required from them and the demand for new competencies. They fear reality because they recognize the status quo has ended and the new model has begun. They resist the transition because they find themselves leaving the comfort of the neutral zone and suddenly lack confidence.

In the context of the modern learning environment, this phase requires school-based leaders to continue to communicate the vision of the modern learning environment, while providing models and exemplars to eliminate ambiguity. It also requires leaders to establish a step by step professional learning plan that provides new training opportunities for everyone involved. Leaders must make it clear that everyone plays an important role in the transition, and as such, they require ongoing support to reach long-term goals. And perhaps most importantly, given the duration of the effort and the likelihood of experiencing fatigue, leaders must celebrate the small wins. They must recognize progress and provide recognition to ensure stakeholders remain engaged, motivated, and fulfilled to sustain what invariably embodies a long, challenging, albeit rewarding journey.

Change management requires school-based leaders to guide teacher leaders and instructional coaches, teachers, students, and parents through the three phases of transition. It calls for school-based leaders to critically think in three separate areas: Resources and training, professional learning, and instructional growth.

··· Resources and Training ···

Resources and training remain fundamental tools in managing the transitional process any substantial change brings. How we allocate resources and use training can delay, and in some cases, prevent people from reaching Bridges' new beginning. Instead, they may find themselves steeped in fear, confusion, grief, and so forth. This only underscores the need for school-based leaders to know how, where, and when to allocate resources and training to ease the transition process. It requires them to evaluate how they currently allocate these resources in the following areas:

- *Professional learning communities*
- *Department and grade level meetings*

- *Staff meetings*
- *Instructional Leadership teams*
- *District professional learning days*
- *School improvement days*
- *Committees*

School-based leaders must become proficient in understanding how to harness resources and training in these areas. They must learn how to use these tools to their advantage to alleviate the psychological burden of change that can undermine or facilitate success.

⋯ Professional Learning ⋯

Professional learning clarifies what otherwise remains opaque and misunderstood. And serves as one of the most powerful tools in any change movement. School-based leaders must leverage professional learning to support teachers in becoming proficient in the modern learning environment. But first they must set the context for professional learning to truly see value from it. Without context, stakeholders enter the learning environment confused, fearful, and disoriented—and ultimately, the outcome of professional learning suffers. Part of their disorientation stems from anxiety as they are thrust into an unknown situation without clarification or explanation. Part of its also stems from a knowledge barrier in key terminology, such as personalized learning or digital curriculum, which serve as jargon for anyone unversed in the modern learning environment. For all these reasons, school-based leaders must invest in professional learning by engaging in several key activities to ensure a smooth and successful transition:

- *Explicitly connect the professional learning to the district's instructional model.*
- *Have teachers identify which part of the district's instructional model they are working to become proficient in.*
- *Allow participants to process the information that they, as facilitators, have provided. Participants need time for conversation and reflection.*
- *Foster a common vocabulary around the modern learning environment that facilitates communication and dialogue.*

School-based leaders cannot and should not be expected to perform these tasks without becoming proficient in the methods that bring about their success. For this reason, this remains an important aspect of their professional learning in change management.

··· Instructional Growth ···

There remains a great difference between ensuring teachers become aware of the modern learning environment, versus training them to become proficient in facilitating it. School-based leaders must prepare and equip teachers to gain the level of knowledge, confidence, and skill to ensure students receive the most value from the new model. This calls for school-based leaders to become proficient in several key areas:

- *Support teachers defining the important thinking skills students must use in the modern learning environment.*
- *Assist teachers in determining the role these skills play as they begin architecting the modern learning environment.*
- *Provide teachers time to reflect on important teaching behaviors by recognizing high-impact activities and providing feedback.*

This serves as the last component of the professional learning school-based leaders receive to become proficient in change management. Ultimately, it prepares them to guide stakeholders through the three phases of transition most efficiently and effectively, and least painfully. School-based leaders, given the importance and nature of their role, must reach a proficiency tipping point sooner than teachers and instructional coaches. While half of all leaders should become proficient by Stage 3, they must reach the tipping point by Stage 4 to establish the conditions needed to support effective and sustainable change throughout the school district.

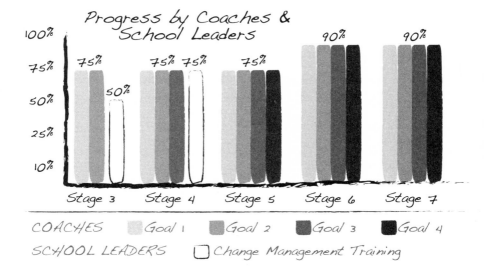

Progress by Coaches & School Leaders

COACHES — Goal 1, Goal 2, Goal 3, Goal 4

SCHOOL LEADERS — Change Management Training

School-based Leader Proficiency –
Change Management

Stage 3:

50% of workforce becomes proficient in Change Management

TIPPING POINT GOALS 1 & 2

Stage 4:

75% of workforce becomes proficient in Change Management

PART III:

THE FRAMEWORK:
Stages 4 and 5

The Framework: Stages 4 and 5

In Stage 4 and 5, you begin to see the institutionalization of the modern learning environment. As you enter Stage 4, the Digital Convergence Framework becomes increasingly important to track and understand your district's progress toward the modern learning environment. You district should strive for the Shape of Change we explored in Part II, which ensures progress in the different drivers remains appropriately distributed to ultimately scale professional learning with the appropriate leadership, instructional, and technological systems in place.

The Journey Continues

You spent the last year developing the conditions for the modern learning environment. You sought answers to questions such as "How do you move your district forward?" and "How do you engage in this work?" In Stages 4 and 5, the questions change and so does your focus as a leader. Rather than catalyzing the effort, your focus shifts toward sustaining attention and focus. How do you continue to maintain your progress? And how do you scale this effort to finally see outcomes in the classroom? These become the key questions in Stages 4 and 5, which you learn through the natural process of working through the Digital Convergence Framework.

STAGE 4

LEADERSHIP
Stage 4

Consider what you just accomplished. In Stage 3 Leadership, you highlighted the achievements of your district, engaged your school-based leaders by educating them, developed systems for long-term, ongoing communication, and began collecting metrics for evaluating progress. Your school-based leaders became prepared to champion the effort in their schools, facilitating the difference between first and second order change for instance, as well as facilitating culture conversations.

Stage 4 requires something different of you. Given the time and amount of work that brought your district to this point, it becomes increasingly important for you to ensure everyone remains focused and committed to the work. The numerous details and shifting priorities may cause stakeholders to lose sight of the broader purpose of their work—the vision of the modern learning environment. This calls for you to constantly and consistently remind them of the ultimate objective of their work and how it fits together.

Stage 4 also requires you to develop the appropriate systems to ensure the integrity of the modern learning environment as you scale it across your organization. This entails developing mechanisms to ensure teachers become proficient in the new modern learning environment.

Ultimately, Stage 4 Leadership sets the conditions for evaluating the effectiveness of professional learning when teachers begin taking it.

Success Indicator #56:
Relentlessly pursue Digital Convergence excellence

Digital Convergence entails a long-term effort that requires sustained focus, commitment, and energy. Stakeholders look to you—their leader—to provide direction. For this reason, you achieve a key success indicator when your messaging promotes a relentless pursuit of Digital Convergence excellence, as well as when you continue to recognize and celebrate the contributions of your stakeholders toward the realization of the desired vision. The journey toward modern learning calls for ongoing motivation, commitment, accountability, and inspiration, all of which requires leaders to ask more of their stakeholders while praising their success.

Success Indicator #57:
Participate in "problems of practice" inquiry

As your district prepares to scale the modern learning environment, you must establish systems to ensure you are continually learning as an organization. This calls for you and your school-based leadership to participate in "problems of practice" inquiry. This focuses on four critical questions through the lens of the newly defined instructional model.

1. *What is the teacher doing or saying?*
2. *What are the students doing or saying?*
3. *What is the instructional task?*
4. *What is the role of technology in the lesson?*

Success Indicator #58:

Align new instructional model with teacher evaluations

To ensure success, you must also evaluate performance through the lens of the new instructional model. You demonstrate another success indicator when you align the new instructional model with teacher evaluations. This success indicator serves an important function, since teachers need to clearly understand what is expected of them, creating transparency that eliminates confusion and resistance, while also promotes accountability.

Choose Your Own Adventure

Digital Convergence occurs non-linearly, requiring work across the five drivers of Leadership, Instructional Models, Modern Curriculum, Digital Ecosystem, and Professional Learning. If you want to read about the success indicators for Leadership Stage 5, refer to page 96. To read about the next driver in Stage 4, continue reading here.

INSTRUCTIONAL MODELS
STAGE 4

In Stage 3, your instructional models team began to gather feedback from instructional staff about the newly defined instructional model and make refinements as appropriate. It served to improve the model, but also to facilitate additional participation, engagement, and ownership of it. Entering Stage 4, your instructional models team begins focusing on creating the conditions for personalized learning to effectively occur. It entails the process of figuring out how to provide learning that accounts for the unique factors of each student, while creating paths that enable students to drive their own learning and provide remediation or acceleration when students need it.

Success Indicator #59:
Re-examine the instructional model

Your district demonstrates another success indicator when your instructional models team re-examines the instructional model to include a continuum of learning for all students in all courses. You also demonstrate the success indicator when your district focuses on the explicit use of the learner profile. If you recall, learner profiles create the condition for personalized learning identifying student learning preferences and style, as well as other leading indicators of how they learn best. Both elements of the success indicator create the conditions for personalized learning to effectively and sustainably occur.

Choose Your Own Adventure

Digital Convergence occurs non-linearly, requiring work across the five drivers of Leadership, Instructional Models, Modern Curriculum, Digital Ecosystem, and Professional Learning. If you want to read about the success indicators for Instructional Models Stage 5, refer to page 98. To read about the next driver in Stage 4, continue reading here.

MODERN CURRICULUM
STAGE 4

In Stage 3 Modern Curriculum, your district developed blended units, made them available in your digital ecosystem, and developed plans to address gaps in digital content. In Stage 4, the focus shifts from creation to refinement. Stage 4 calls for ensuring curriculum continues to provide optimal value and relevance for students over time, accounting for their personalized needs.

Success Indicator #60:

Modernizing the district's curriculum

Your district demonstrates a success indicator when the modernization of your curriculum continues to evolve, with a greater focus on personalized learning. Like Stage 4 Instructional Models, this prepares your district to effectively and sustainably offer personalized learning to students.

── Choose Your Own Adventure ──

Digital Convergence occurs non-linearly, requiring work across the five drivers of Leadership, Instructional Models, Modern Curriculum, Digital Ecosystem, and Professional Learning. If you want to read about the success indicators for Modern Curriculum Stage 5, refer to page 100. To read about the next driver in Stage 4, continue reading here.

DIGITAL ECOSYSTEM
STAGE 4

In Stage 3, the digital ecosystems team focused on establishing a cadence and rhythm for working on integration needs, monitoring progress, and reviewing milestones continuously. The team also established a hierarchal rollout plan of the ecosystem to user groups. In Stage 4, the team focuses on establishing the conditions to support the expansion of the digital ecosystem into the classroom. It requires ensuring that technology becomes integrated within the ecosystem, allowing for a seamless experience for teachers and students. And it also entails establishing a routine process for evaluating systems.

Success Indicator #61:

Gain commitment of vendor partners

The digital ecosystems team demonstrates a success indicator when it gets vendors to become partners of the ecosystem. All vendors that make up the district's digital ecosystem contractually commit to the integration work and standards or provide the district a timeline for additional development needs. This lays the foundation for interoperability among otherwise disparate systems.

Success Indicator #62:

Establish protocols for regular testing of information systems

The digital ecosystems team also demonstrates another success indicator when it establishes protocols for regular testing (quality assurance) of information systems, and ensures user access continues to be evaluated after any unforeseen updates and/or bugs. Both promote the accessibility and availability of the digital ecosystem, while maintaining its integrity.

Choose Your Own Adventure

Digital Convergence occurs non-linearly, requiring work across the five drivers of Leadership, Instructional Models, Modern Curriculum, Digital Ecosystem, and Professional Learning. If you want to read about the success indicators for Digital Ecosystem Stage 5, refer to page 101. To read about the next driver in Stage 4, continue reading here.

PROFESSIONAL LEARNING
STAGE 4

Professional Learning in Stage 3 focused on deploying professional learning programs. The professional learning team assessed and monitored all programs for effectiveness, as well as helped some school-based leaders, instructional coaches, and the teacher cohort achieve proficiency in the modern learning environment per their role. Stage 4 focuses on scaling professional learning to all teachers, making sure instructional coaches and school-based leaders become ready to support teachers, and beginning to evaluate the impact of professional learning on student outcomes.

Success Indicator #63:

A critical mass of school-based leadership completes change management professional learning

Your district demonstrates a success indicator when a critical mass (75 percent) of school-based leadership complete the "Change Management for School Leaders" module. As we explored in Part II, school-based leaders must become proficient in change management to effectively address stakeholder concerns and ensure their schools match the direction and pace of change of the overall district.

Success Indicator #64:

A critical mass of coaches achieves district's PL Goal 3

Your district demonstrates a success indicator when a critical mass (75 percent) of coaches achieve the district's PL Goal 3. If you recall, the four professional learning goals your district creates describes the ability teachers need to acquire, the outcome they need to achieve, and the extent of their achievement. Achieving this success indicator ensures a system of coaches is available to support teachers as they engage in professional learning activities.

Success Indicator #65:

10 percent of teachers achieve district's PL Goal 3

When 10 percent of teachers achieve the district's PL Goal 3, your district demonstrates a success indicator. Teachers begin to become proficient in the third professional learning goal, acquiring the skills and competencies they need to achieve goals relative to your district's defined instructional model.

Success Indicator #66:

10 percent of teachers achieve district's PL Goal 4

This success indicators continues to advance the abilities of teachers and   occurs when 10 percent of teachers achieve the district's PL Goal 4.

Success Indicator #67:

30 percent of teachers achieve district's PL Goal 1

In Stage 3, 10 percent of teachers achieved your district's PL Goal 1. In Stage 4, you demonstrate a success indicator when that number climbs to 30 percent.

Success Indicator #68:

30 percent of teachers achieve district's PL Goal 2

Like the previous success indicator, your district experiences a success indicator when 30 percent of teachers achieve the districts PL Goal 2.

Success Indicator #69:

Track and monitor student outcome metrics

A key focus is to understand the effectiveness of professional learning as more teachers participate in it. Your district demonstrates a success indicator when it begins to track and monitor student outcome metrics going beyond quantitative state assessments. This ensures that you begin to assess teaching and learning outside the realm of traditional testing.

Choose Your Own Adventure

Digital Convergence occurs non-linearly, requiring work across the five drivers of Leadership, Instructional Models, Modern Curriculum, Digital Ecosystem, and Professional Learning. If you want to read about the success indicators for Professional Learning Stage 5, refer to page 102. To read about the Leadership in Stage 5, continue reading here.

STAGE 5

LEADERSHIP
STAGE 5

In Leadership Stage 5, you continue to focus on ensuring stakeholders remain committed, engaged, and aligned in the movement toward the modern learning environment. Increasingly, your focus during this stage falls on refining the systems for promoting accountability and measuring effectiveness. You also continue to facilitate others to champion the change.

Success Indicator #70:
Message the need to sustain effort

When your messaging serves the purpose of keeping stakeholders focused and accountable, while also motivated and satisfied, you demonstrate another success indicator. Your messaging reflects the need for the organization to monitor, learn and adjust its Digital Convergence plans. Both through your efforts and others, progress continues to be continuously communicated, while the district keeps its "eye on the prize."

Success Indicator #71:

Finalize teacher evaluation

Building off the work of Stage 4, you demonstrate another success indicator when you finalize the updated teacher evaluation and ensure it aligns to the district's new instructional model. Through this process, you finalize an effective system of measurement and accountability that ultimately leads to better student outcomes and teacher satisfaction and engagement.

Success Indicator #72:

Move from awareness to action

97

While in Stage 4, you and school-based leadership participated in "problems of practice" inquiry, school-based leaders and teacher leaders take the responsibility going into Stage 5. School-based and teacher leaders move from awareness to action, while "problems of practice" (Instructional Rounds) are ongoing. School-based action plans are developed for school wide improvement. All efforts continue to scale accountability and evaluation beyond the district level to the school and classroom level.

Success Indicator #73:

Sustain recognition of progress

Your district achieves another success indicator when formal and informal celebrations and recognition become pervasive throughout the district culture. Recognition remains an important need, since it fosters a sense of renewed commitment and motivation to the ultimate vision of the modern learning environment.

INSTRUCTIONAL MODELS
STAGE 5

Instructional Models Stage 5 builds on the progress of Stage 4 in developing systems to support personalized learning. During this stage, the instructional models team develops further processes and tools that facilitate personalized learning, including learner profiles as well as the sequence and scope of learning for students. It also begins to implement the new instructional model in the district.

Success Indicator #74:
Research and identify a continuum of learning and learner profiles

Your district demonstrates a success indicator when the instructional models team researches, identifies, and clearly defines a continuum of learning and learner profiles. It also experiences the success indicator when it includes both as part of the Instructional Model.

Success Indicator #75:
Identify and procure a tool for assessing learner profiles

In addition to defining learner profiles, the instructional models team experiences another success indicator when it identifies and procures a tool for assessing learner profiles. The tool ensures that learner profiles continue to add appropriate and sustainable value for students over time.

Success Indicator #76:
Provide blended courses at high-school level and empower teachers to manage instructional time

In Stage 5, the district begins to see the rollout of the new instructional model and modern curriculum. It demonstrates another success indicator when the district offers some blended courses at the high school level and empowers teachers to make informed decisions regarding instructional time with students.

MODERN CURRICULUM
STAGE 5

Moving into Modern Curriculum Stage 5, students gain the ability to demonstrate the expertise they acquired from their learning. Unlike state assessments, they also acquire the ability to demonstrate the effectiveness of their learning according to their individual preferences and needs.

Success Indicator #77:
Ensure all subjects and courses enable students to demonstrate mastery

The district demonstrates a success indicator when all subjects and courses provide opportunities for students to demonstrate mastery along a continuum of learning that includes student choice and problem-solving within an authentic context. This enables students to acquire and demonstrate expertise as they navigate their continuum of learning. Students can demonstrate their learning by choosing the method that reflects their learning style, such as visually, verbally, or kinesthetically. Students also gain the opportunity to demonstrate their learning in an authentic context, such as applying their knowledge through meaningful activities rather than traditional testing.

DIGITAL ECOSYSTEMS
Stage 5

Entering Stage 5, the digital ecosystems team works to solidify the accessibility and availability for the district's ecosystem. Conceptually, it enables the ecosystem to support its sustainable use as a living, breathing habitat that facilitates the personalized, modern learning environment.

Success Indicator #78:
Identify and review all data to exchange and cross-reference user profiles

Another success indicator occurs when the district's digital ecosystems team identifies and reviews all data that needs to be shared across the systems and subsystems of the ecosystem, and cross-references user profiles (user access levels) to ensure users gain access to the data sets they need.

PROFESSIONAL LEARNING
STAGE 5

In Professional Learning Stage 5, we see the district establish a proficiency tipping point for PL goals 1 and 2, as well as the tipping point for instructional coaches for PL Goal 4.

Success Indicator #79:

A critical mass of coaches achieves district's PL Goal 4

The district demonstrates a success indicator when a critical mass (75%) of coaches achieve the district's PL Goal 4. Achieving this success indicator ensures a system of coaches is prepared to support teachers as they work to become proficient in the fourth professional learning goal.

Success Indicator #80:

30 percent of teachers achieve district's PL Goal 3

When 30 percent of the district's teachers achieve PL Goal 3, the district demonstrates a success indicator.

Success Indicator #81:

30 percent of teachers achieve district's PL Goal 4

Like the previous success indicator, 30 percent of the

district's teachers must achieve PL Goal 4 to experience this success indicator.

Success Indicator #82:

60 percent of teachers achieve district's PL Goal 1

Once 60 percent of the district's teachers achieve the district's PL Goal 1, they experience a success indicator. This represents the proficiency tipping point for Goal 1.

Success Indicator #83:

60 percent of teachers achieve district's PL Goal 2

For PL Goal 2, teachers also reach the proficiency tipping point when 60 percent achieve it, which demonstrates another success indicator.

Success Indicator #84:

Continue tracking and monitoring student outcome metrics

Expanding upon the metrics in Stage 4, the district demonstrates another success indicator when it tracks and monitors student outcome metrics and ensures alignment to its Theory of Action, Vision and Instructional Model.

104

CONCLUSION

Recall in Part I when we discussed *The Tipping Point: How Little Things Can Make a Big Difference*. Malcolm Gladwell writes about the phenomenon of when epidemics quickly spread—social movements, diseases, etc.—given conditions and small events that set them in motion. Yet our focus on the tipping point has largely centered on the time before and shortly after this phenomenon. We explored, for instance, how your district set the conditions for personalized, modern learning to occur effectively and sustainably in the classroom. Using Gladwell's "three rules of a Tipping Point," we explored how the Law of the Few, the Stickiness Factor, and the Power of Context enabled you to create an early movement toward 21st century teaching and learning that built positive inertia.

And then we turned our attention to the importance of scaling those conditions in the classroom, ensuring school-based leaders, coaches, and teachers became proficient in the modern learning environment. But largely, our focus stopped there. Yet what lies ahead represents the most fruitful and exciting work in our journey. Stage 6 and 7 turn our attention from creating to leveraging the modern learning environment to improve student outcomes on a scale and depth never achieved before.

In *The New Agenda*, we defined the purpose of K–12 public education since its founding. Our school systems emerged to answer society's call to produce graduates competent and capable of meeting the needs of the time. Before the emergence of the digital age, K–12 education could answer this call and keep pace with society. On the one hand, innovation occurred slowly compared with what we see today. On the other, the world operated in an analog environment that promoted silos among systems and entities, schools and society included. Yet that all changed with the rise of digital technology, which not only made silos obsolete, but unsustainable. And while most industries and enterprises evolved to meet the new demands of the digital world, K–12 did not. For the first time, we witnessed our school systems become misaligned with the realities and conditions of the external environment. The rate of technological change outpaced our ability to keep up.

In Stage 6 and 7, we see this trend reverse as our school systems restore alignment with society. The modern learning environment enables districts to synchronize with the external world and therefore produce graduates prepared to compete in today's era. While the entire Digital Convergence Framework focuses on breaking down silos, Stages 6 and 7 truly integrate and embed the modern learning environment with the digital world to sustain value over time. This remains essential given the rapid changes we see now.

So, as industries increasingly focus on using information to drive greater value and performance, Stage 6 and 7 enable K–12 to do the same. Ultimately, these stages enable K–12 to transform the process of Digital Convergence into a science. *The Science of Convergence*—what represents the next phase of this journey—calls for continually testing, measuring, evaluating, and optimizing how we provide and sustain value to our students, teachers, and other stakeholders. How? By leveraging the power of information. As we transition into Stage 6 and 7, we begin to understand Convergence as a science, as teachers, students, and stakeholders become producers and consumers of information via the digital ecosystem. At these stages, the ecosystem truly becomes a living, breathing habitat, where users exchange information over the network at a rate and frequency to produce a wealth of new knowledge that can inform better solutions. These solutions don't exist in a vacuum; rather, they directly apply to the world existing beyond the physical structure of the traditional school system.

Imagine the value of understanding the direct relationship between technology and learning, enabling you to articulate the interrelationship regularly with teachers, students, and other stakeholders.

Imagine gaining the ability to continuously examine your Instructional Model against the needs of society, and update it as needed to produce the best outcomes for students.

Imagine the value of gaining access to a dynamic instructional infrastructure that adapts to the best practices in instruction and most effective curriculum.

Imagine the value of leveraging a technological infrastructure, one that integrates with new and emerging technologies to unlock new value in an instructional context.

Imagine gaining full transparency and metrics showing the impact of Digital Convergence on student outcomes. Or imagine the benefit of continually updating professional learning to reflect the emerging best pedagogical practices.

These are not imaginings, but realities of Stage 6 and 7. Once we reach these stages, we not only reach modern learning at scale, but begin to measure, extend, and sustain its impact.

Today, our team is actively working with major research institutions across the U.S. to bring a coherent science to digital convergence. As more districts progress through the stages of the Digital Convergence Framework we gain greater insights into this work.

The journey toward Digital Convergence is a long and arduous one. However, I remain more optimistic and committed to this work than ever before. The real value of our collective progress exists within our grasp.

Onward, forward.

Appendix

DIGITAL CONVERGENCE FRAMEWORK

———————— E M E R G I N G ————————

STAGE 1

Leadership

1. Message from the Top (MFTT) — The superintendent has communicated the desire to leverage technology to trans- form teaching and learning and has invited all stakeholders to co-construct the vision of the modern learning environment
2. Cross-functional team has been formed and serves as the district's Digital Convergence Steering Committee
3. A Theory of Action has been developed for the transforma- tion of teaching and learning through Digital Convergence
4. Stakeholders have been identified and engaged in activities around the Theory of Action and the construction of the vision of the modern learning environment

Instructional Models

5. Cross-functional team has been formed to explore new instructional models, with one team member designated as the owner
6. Cross-functional team begins conversations about a newly defined instructional model, including use of learner pro- files, blended and personalized learning and a competency- based education system
7. Cross-functional team begins conversations about adopting a framework for assessing instructional rigor
8. Cross-functional team begins conversations about adopting a framework for 21st century skills

Modern Curriculum

9. The district is beginning to explore a common blended unit plan across all subjects, courses, and grade levels

Digital Ecosystems

10. Cross-functional team is formed to explore the district's digital ecosystem. One person is designated as the owner
11. District begins conversations about its digital ecosystem including its purpose, users, systems, subsystems, and functions, and how it will support and align to the district's instructional model

Professional Learning

12. Cross-functional team is formed to develop, deploy, and monitor the district's professional learning and growth as it relates to Digital Convergence, with one team member designated as the owner

111

STAGE 2

Leadership

13. Message from the Top — The superintendent has communicated to stakeholders the successful development of the vision of the modern learning environment
14. Modern Learning Environment Vision Deck has been developed and delivered to all stakeholders
15. District common language glossary of terms has been developed and published with a plan to maintain and update over time
16. A district brand for Digital Convergence has been defined
17. The work of Digital Convergence is aligned to your district's strategic plan

Instructional Models

18. District-wide instructional model defined
19. Agreed upon framework for assessing instructional rigor
20. Agreed upon framework for assessing twenty-first century skills

Modern Curriculum

21. The district has conducted an assessment of its digital content, including its purchased content and where teachers are accessing free content
22. A common blended unit plan that is aligned with the new instructional model has been developed by the district across all subjects, courses, and grade levels
23. Model digital/blended lessons have been developed, are aligned with the new instructional model, and are available inside the district's digital ecosystem

Digital Ecosystems

24. The technical build of the district's digital ecosystem begins while integration needs, progress monitoring, and milestones are continuously reviewed
25. The district has defined the digital ecosystem's systems, subsystems, and their functions
26. The district has procured a learning management system as part of their digital ecosystem
27. The district extends the brand of Digital Convergence to its ecosystem, including a name for the ecosystem, stakeholder communication, and visuals to represent the conceptual design
28. The district has conducted an assessment of its instructional digital tools, including both purchased tools and high access free tools

Professional Learning

29. The district has identified a professional learning implementation model with the necessary resources to support its success
30. Coaches to support Digital Convergence have been identified consistent with the district's implementation model
31. A professional learning plan has been developed consistent with the district's implementation model (SI29) and includes professional learning goals aligned to the district's newly defined instructional model (SI 18 & 41)
32. A critical mass (75%) of coaches of Digital Convergence are ready and prepared with the knowledge, materials, and time

to support the initial cohort launch

33. An initial group of teachers are selected and grouped in professional learning cohorts consistent with the district's implementation model

34. Coaches of Digital Convergence have kicked off their teacher cohorts with a face-to-face session where they set expectations, build awareness of tools and resources, and generate excitement for the journey ahead

STAGE 3

Leadership

35. Message from the Top — The superintendent has communicated to all stakeholders the key wins in Digital Convergence during the first two stages, and continues to update all stakeholders with next steps in the work

36. All school-based leaders have been trained on leading change (i.e. change management theory, first and second order change)

37. School-based plans have been created for "culture conversations"

38. School-based leaders have facilitated "culture conversations" around Digital Convergence and the need to transform teaching and learning

39. Plans to communicate the work of Digital Convergence (internally and externally) through various media outlets are continuous and on-going

40. Establish metrics aligned to the theory of action and formalize a reflection process

Instructional Models

41. The new instructional model has defined identifiers, a timeline for launching to stakeholders, and alignment to teacher professional learning

Modern Curriculum

42. Model blended units have been developed, are aligned to the new instructional model, and are available inside the district's digital ecosystem

43. The district has identified gaps in digital content across all subjects, courses, and grade levels and has a plan to address the gap

Digital Ecosystems

44. Regular cadence has been established for the digital ecosystem Team while integration needs, progress monitoring, and milestones are continuously reviewed
45. A hierarchical rollout to stakeholder groups has been defined and a go-live date has been set first for internal testing, and then tiered access

Professional Learning

46. School-based leadership begins to engage in the professional learning content aligned to the district's Instructional Model
47. Professional learning plans have been developed for new teacher induction and include a pathway for all new teachers to reach proficiency in the goals set in the district's Professional Learning plan within the first three years of their employment
48. Coaches of Digital Convergence professional learning is in progress with clear evidence that the team continuously monitors effectiveness based upon a number of data points
49. Teacher cohort professional learning is in progress, with clear evidence that the team continuously monitors effectiveness based upon a number of data points
50. Fifty percent of school-based leadership have completed the "Change Management for School Leaders" module
51. A critical mass (75%) of coaches of Digital Convergence have achieved the district's PL Goal 1
52. A critical mass (75%) of coaches of Digital Convergence have achieved the district's PL Goal 2
53. Ten percent of the district's teachers have achieved the district's PL Goal 1
54. Ten percent of the district's teachers have achieved the district's PL Goal 2

55. The district begins to talk about student outcome metrics going beyond quantitative state assessments

---
GOOD

STAGE 4
Leadership
56. Message from the Top — Messaging reflects a relentless pursuit of Digital Convergence excellence. Wins are celebrated during the first four stages, while continuously focusing all stakeholders towards the realization of the desired vision
57. District leadership and school-based leadership participate in "problems of practice" inquiry (Instructional rounds) based upon 4 critical questions: What is the teacher doing or saying? What are the students doing or saying? What is the instructional task? What is the role of technology in the lesson? These questions tie back to the district's newly defined instructional model
58. District leadership begins to align new instructional model with teacher evaluations

Instructional Models
59. The district re-examines its instructional model to include a continuum of learning for all students in all courses as well the explicit use of learner profile

Modern Curriculum
60. Modernization of the district's curriculum continues to evolve over time, with key consideration of personalized learning

Digital Ecosystems
61. All vendors that make up the district's digital ecosystem have contractually committed to the integration work/standards or provided the district a timeline for additional development needs
62. Protocols have been established for regular testing (QA) of

115

information systems and user access to the ecosystem as a result of any unforeseen updates and/or bugs

Professional Learning

63. A critical mass (75%) of School-based leadership have completed the "Change Management for School Leaders" module
64. A critical mass (75%) of coaches of Digital Convergence have achieved the district's PL Goal 3
65. Ten percent of the district's teachers have achieved the district's PL Goal 3
66. Ten percent of the district's teachers have achieved the district's PL Goal 4
67. Thirty percent of the district's teachers have achieved the district's PL Goal 1
68. Thirty percent of the district's teachers have achieved the district's PL Goal 2
69. The district begins to track and monitor student outcome metrics going beyond quantitative state assessments

STAGE 5

Leadership

70. Message from the Top — Messaging reflects the need for the organization to monitor, learn and adjust its Digital Convergence plans. Wins are continuously communicated while keeping the "eye on the prize"
71. District leadership has finalized the updated teacher evaluation, in alignment with the district's new instructional model
72. School-based and teacher leaders move from awareness to action, while "problems of practice" (Instructional Rounds) are ongoing. School-based action plans are developed for school-wide improvement
73. Formal and informal celebrations and recognition are pervasive throughout the district culture

Instructional Models

74. A continuum of learning and learner profiles have been researched, are clearly defined, and are part of the Instructional Model
75. A tool for assessing learner profiles is identified and procured
76. Some courses at the high school level are blended and teachers are empowered to make informed decisions regarding instructional time with students

Modern Curriculum

77. All subjects and courses have opportunities for students to demonstrate mastery along a continuum of learning that includes student choice and problem-solving within an authentic context

Digital Ecosystems

78. The district's digital ecosystem team has identified and reviewed all data that needs to be shared across the systems and subsystems of the ecosystem. Further, user profiles (user access levels) have been cross-referenced to ensure users have access to the data sets they need

Professional Learning

79. A critical mass (75%) of coaches of Digital Convergence have achieved the district's PL Goal 4
80. Thirty percent of the district's teachers have achieved the district's PL Goal 3
81. Thirty percent of the district's teachers have achieved the district's PL Goal 4
82. Sixty percent of the district's teachers have achieved the district's PL Goal 1
83. Sixty percent of the district's teachers have achieved the district's PL Goal 2
84. The district continues to track and monitor student outcome metrics by expanding upon the metrics in Stage 4 and ensuring alignment to their Theory of Action, Vision, and Instructional Model

STAGE 6

Leadership

85. Message from the Top — Messaging reflects the district's stature as a model district based upon the hard work of all stakeholders. It reminds people of the focused work to get where they are, with a nudge to the future work ahead

86. The district's strategic plan is continuously examined with clear evidence of monitoring, updates, and adjustments documented

Instructional Models

87. Students progress through curriculum only after mastery, and the district's grading policies are updated appropriately to reflect this progression

88. All students are assessed for their learner profile and are aware of "how they learn"

89. Students are grouped based upon characteristics in their learner profile, rather than their age or grade level

90. Students have choice over the time, place, path, and pace of their learning

91. All courses at the high school level are blended and teachers are empowered to make informed decisions regarding instructional time with students

Modern Curriculum

92. The district's curriculum is continuously examined and monitored against the needs of society

Digital Ecosystems

93. A continuous feedback loop has been established between the district's digital ecosystem and all end user groups. Feedback is prioritized into an actionable development roadmap for the ecosystem

Professional Learning

94. Clear evidence exists that the professional learning team

has fostered cross-collaboration opportunities among teachers that includes opportunities to observe and provide peer-to-peer feedback and support within one's own school and across schools. There is a deep sense of reflection and practice with the key deliverable moving from fluency to mastery in Digital Convergence

95. Ninety percent of coaches of Digital Convergence have achieved all district PL Goals
96. Sixty percent of the district's teachers have achieved the district's PL Goal 3
97. Sixty percent of the district's teachers have achieved the district's PL Goal 4
98. Ninety percent of the district's teachers have achieved the district's PL Goal 1
99. Ninety percent of the district's teachers have achieved the district's PL Goal 2
100. The district begins to schedule performance meetings at all levels of the organization to review data on the impact of Digital Convergence and student outcomes

STAGE 7

Leadership

101. Message from the Top — District leadership communicates with all stakeholders on a regular basis about the ever-changing landscape of technology and how it affects learning
102. The district's vision is updated to reflect the new needs of society

Instructional Models

103. The district's instructional model is continuously examined against the needs of society and best practices for learning. As technology adapts and changes, the district refines their instructional model to meet these needs

Modern Curriculum

104. District curriculum is updated "just in time" by utilizing its technology tools and digital ecosystem

Digital Ecosystems

105. The district's digital ecosystem has become a multi-vendor, interconnected and interactive tool that meets the needs of a diverse group of stakeholders. As new technologies become available the ecosystem is nimble enough to integrate these tools within the structures of the ecosystem

Professional Learning

106. Professional learning team continuously monitors curriculum adjustments, technology upgrades/changes, and best practices for instructional design and delivery and has a systemic plan to update training content and modules on a continuous basis

107. The district has regularly scheduled performance meetings at all levels of the organization to review data on the impact of Digital Convergence and student outcomes

108. Ninety percent of the district's teachers have achieved the district's PL Goal 3

109. Ninety percent of the district's teachers have achieved the district's PL Goal 4

110. District defined student outcomes metric here

CITATIONS

Bridges, William. *Managing Transitions: Making the Most of Change.* Philadelphia: De Capo Lifelong Books, 2009.

Fred, Charles. *Breakaway.* New York: Jossey-Bass, 2002.

Gladwell, Malcolm. *The Tipping Point: How Little Things Can Make a Big Difference.* New York: Little, Brown and Company, 2002.

"Human Capital 30: Companies that Put Employees Front and Center." *Fortune.* Accessed January 17, 2018. http://fortune.com/2016/03/08/human-capital-30/

"Hyatt." *Fortune.* Accessed January 17, 2018. http://fortune.com/best-companies/hyatt/

Smith, Shawn. *The New Agenda: Achieving Personalized Learning Through Digital Convergence.* Denver, Magnusson-Skor Publishing, 2017.

"Stryker." *Fortune.* Accessed January 17, 2018. http://fortune.com/best-companies/stryker/

Rosenbluth, Hal. *The Customer Comes Second: And Other Secrets of Exceptional Service.* New York: William Morrow and Company, 1992.

ABOUT THE AUTHOR

 Dr. Shawn K. Smith is an education futurist and a national leader on issues surrounding digital education and pedagogy and is currently serving as President of Modern Teacher. He is compelled to preserve education's rich heritage and support America's teachers and leaders as they transition traditional classrooms into modern learning environments.

As a rare book collector, Smith has one of the world's largest private collections of John Dewey's writings. He is the author of *Teacher as Architect: Instructional Design and Delivery for the Modern Teacher* and *The New Agenda: Achieving Personalized Learning Through Digital Convergence.* He has appeared on both the Discovery Channel and TLC as well as various radio, web, and podcast programs.

Prior to founding Modern Teacher, Smith was a teacher, principal, and Chief of Schools for 15 years in school districts in Illinois and California. He holds degrees from Carthage College in Kenosha, Wisconsin (bachelor's degree, elementary education), the California State University, San Bernardino (master's degree, middle school education), and the University of Southern California (doctorate degree, urban education policy and leadership).

Dr. Shawn K. Smith's extensive research and experience in the field continues to inform his thought leadership. Today, he collaborates with more than 100 school districts across the country to help them overcome challenges with technology integration. In his role as President of Modern Teacher, he works beside some of today's most innovative and prominent leaders to challenge the status quo and find new, better solutions.

modern
teacher

Modern Teacher.
Transitioning traditional classrooms to modern
learning environments.

Modern Teacher is a National Network of school districts reshaping our American education system by transitioning from traditional classrooms to modern learning environments. Individually, members personalize learning at scale for their districts by progressing through the Digital Convergence Framework housed in Modern Teacher's online platform - connecting districts to the tools and metrics to effectively reach their goals. Collectively, members collaborate on common goals and challenges with educational leaders nationwide to establish best practices and create a united voice for the future of K–12 education.

To learn more about Modern Teacher, visit:
www.modernteacher.com

PUBLISHING, LLC

Magnusson-Skor Publishing.
Exclusively Publishing the Work of Entrepreneurs.

Magnusson-Skor Publishing, an imprint of MSKOR, is the exclusive partner of entrepreneurs seeking a platform to promote their thought leadership. We bring more than a decade of experience helping today's premier business leaders connect with audiences through best-selling books, keynote speeches, online media, and other outlets.

To learn more about MSKOR, visit:

www.mskor.com

DIGITAL CONVERGENCE ASSESSMENT

To learn where your school district stands in the journey toward Digital Convergence, take the Digital Convergence Assessment. This open-source assessment identifies your district's starting point and immediate action items to create a personalized, or modern, learning environment.

To access the assessment, visit
www.modernteacher.com